A Man for All Seasons

Robert Bolt

Guide written and developed by
John Mahoney and Stewart Martin

Charles Letts & Co Ltd
London, Edinburgh & New York

First published 1987
by Charles Letts & Co Ltd
Diary House, Borough Road, London SE1 1DW

Illustration: Peter McClure

The authors and publishers are grateful
to Heinemann Educational Books Ltd
for permission to quote from
A Man for All Seasons by Robert Bolt.

Stewart Martin is an Honours graduate of Lancaster University, where he read English
and Sociology. He has worked both in the UK and abroad as a writer, a teacher, and an
educational consultant. He is married with three children, and is currently deputy
headmaster at Ossett School in West Yorkshire.

John Mahoney has taught English for twenty years. He has been head of English
department in three schools and has wide experience of preparing students at all levels
for most examination boards. He has worked both in the UK and North America
producing educational books and computer software on English language and literature.
He is married with three children and lives in Worcestershire.

British Library Cataloguing in Publication Data
Mahoney, John
  A man for all seasons: Robert Bolt: guide.
  (Guides to literature)
  I. Bolt, Robert, Man for all seasons
  I. Title II. Martin, Stewart III. Bolt,
  Robert. Man for all seasons IV. Series
  822'.914 PR6052.039M33

ISBN 0 85097 770 3

Printed and bound in Great Britain by
Charles Letts (Scotland) Ltd

Contents

To the student

This study companion to your English literature text acts as a guide to the novel or play being studied. It suggests ways in which you can explore content and context, and focuses your attention on those matters which will lead to an understanding, appreciative and sensitive response to the work of literature being studied.

Whilst covering all those aspects dealt with in the traditional-style study aid, more importantly, it is a flexible companion to study, enabling you to organize the patterns of study and priorities which reflect your particular needs at any given moment.

Whilst in many places descriptive, it is never prescriptive, always encouraging a sensitive personal response to a work of literature, rather than the shallow repetition of others' opinions. Such objectives have always been those of the good teacher, and have always assisted the student to gain high grades in 16+ examinations in English literature. These same factors are also relevant to students who are doing coursework in English literature for the purposes of continual assessment.

The major part of this guide is the 'Commentary' where you will find a detailed commentary and analysis of all the important things you should know and study for your examination. There is also a section giving practical help on how to study a set text, write the type of essay that will gain high marks, prepare coursework and a guide to sitting examinations.

Used sensibly, this guide will be invaluable in your studies and help ensure your success in the course.

Most editions of the play do not have scene divisions marked in them. However, they have been included in the guide for clarity and to enable easy reference to the text which you are using. It is fairly obvious from stage directions and the change of subject matter and characters where scene divisions occur.

Robert Bolt

Robert Bolt was born in Manchester in 1922. He left school at sixteen and worked in an office. During and after the war years he was in the armed forces, became a member of, and then left, the Communist party, and studied for a degree in history. In the fifties he engaged in protests against the atom bomb, for which he spent a short time in prison because he refused to be 'bound over to keep the peace', a difficult decision and a distressing experience for a law-abiding citizen. Robert Bolt was a teacher in a Somerset school when his first play, *The Critic and the Heart*, was first produced in Oxford in 1957.

His other plays include *The Flowering Cherry* (1957), *The Tiger and the Horse* (1958), *A Man for All Seasons* (1960), *Gentle Jack* (1963) and *Vivat, Vivat Regina* (1970).

He is also well known as a film-script writer, and wrote the scripts for *Lawrence of Arabia, Doctor Zhivago, Ryan's Daughter, Lady Caroline Lamb* and *The Missionary.* His most successful plays have been *The Flowering Cherry, A Man for All Seasons* and *Vivat, Vivat Regina*, the last two transferring successfully to New York.

In *A Man for All Seasons*, Bolt found a vehicle for theatrical experimentation. Influenced by Brecht, he used an innovative way of presenting multiple scenes which span the last eight years of More's life, using a narrator-figure who changes roles throughout the play in order to depict minor characters.

The play is concerned with a great 16th-century Christian and Catholic who gives up his life for a religious conviction. Bolt admits that he does not share that conviction, not being a Catholic or, indeed, a practising Christian. The author shows the attempts made by Secretary Cromwell's police state to bully More into giving approval to Henry VIII's divorce. The dramas which are played out in the court-room scene, and which are rich in legal quibbling, find no reflection or corresponding struggle in More's soul. There is no doubt in his mind, nor has there ever been, that what he is doing is right.

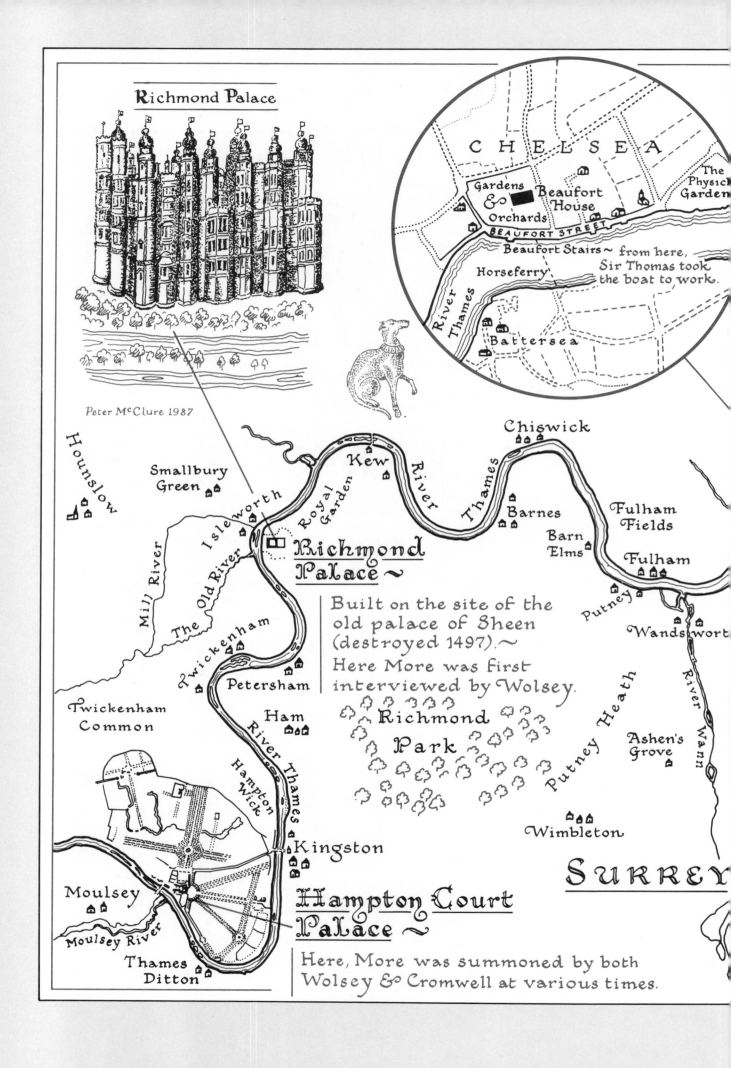

Richmond Palace

Peter McClure 1987

CHELSEA

The Physic Garden

Gardens & Orchards — Beaufort House

BEAUFORT STREET

Beaufort Stairs ~ from here, Sir Thomas took the boat to work.

Horseferry

River Thames

Battersea

Hounslow

Smallbury Green

Chiswick

Kew

River Thames

Royal Garden

Isleworth

Mill River

The Old River

Richmond Palace ~

Built on the site of the old palace of Sheen (destroyed 1497). ~ Here More was first interviewed by Wolsey.

Barnes

Barn Elms

Fulham Fields

Fulham

Putney

Wandsworth

Twickenham

Petersham

Richmond Park

Putney Heath

River Wann

Twickenham Common

Ham

Ashen's Grove

River Thames

Hampton Wick

Wimbleton

Moulsey

Kingston

Hampton Court Palace ~

SURREY

Moulsey River

Thames Ditton

Here, More was summoned by both Wolsey & Cromwell at various times.

The Tower of London

Here, Sir Thomas More was imprisoned, and later executed on 6th. July, 1535.

MOAT

Chapel
Scaffold
White Tower
Old Drawbridge
Roman Bastion
Lion Tower
Bloody Tower
Wakefield Tower
Traitors' Gate

MOAT

LONDON

By this time, already the largest city in Europe with a population of 250,000.

Westminster

Chelsea

Battersea Common Fields

Southwark

The Tower of London

River Thames

Hall of Westminster~

Here, Sir Thomas More's trial took place, beginning on 1st. July, 1535.

Beaufort House

Sir Thomas More's house at Chelsea. It was here that King Henry VIII visited More. Beaufort House stood across what is now Beaufort Street, about half way between Cheyne Walk and the King's Road.
(In More's time, Beaufort St. followed the bank of the River Thames, where now runs Cheyne Walk).
Beaufort House was pulled down in 1740 on the orders of Sir Hans Sloane.

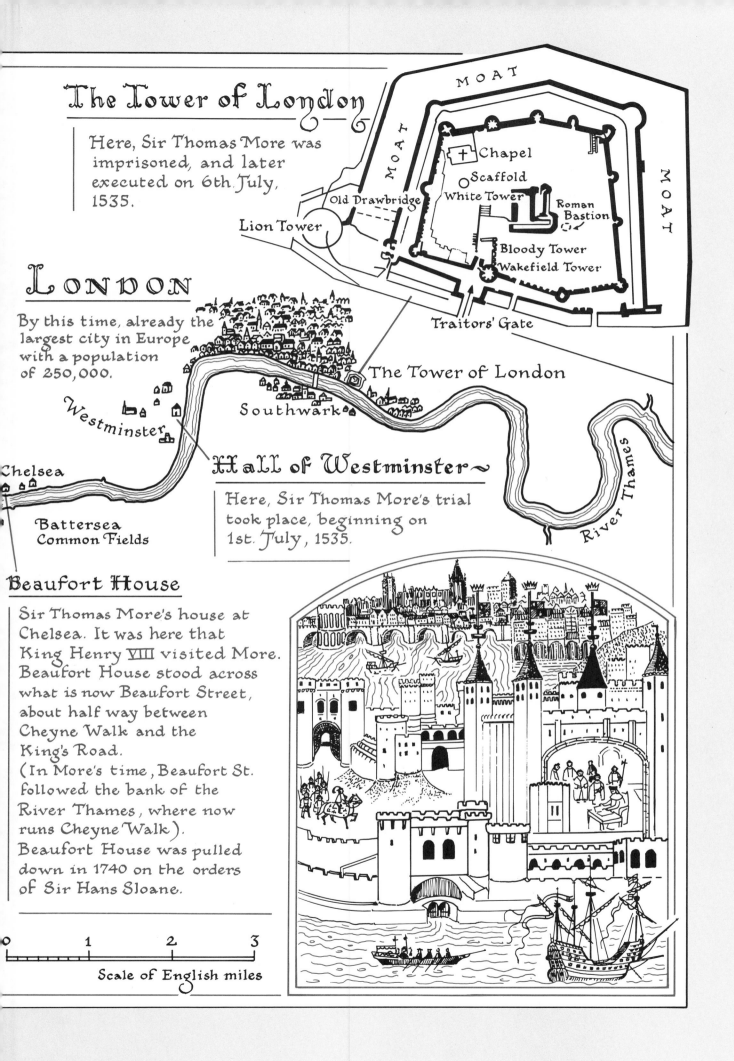

0   1   2   3

Scale of English miles

Understanding
A Man for All Seasons

An exploration of the major topics and themes in the play

The historical context of the play is that period of time when England was at its most intellectually turbulent. Throughout Europe, kings and their subjects alike were attempting to come to terms with matters of belief and religious dogma which were being subject to rigorous investigation and attack. Some of the moral ambiguity of the characters could be seen to stem from this turbulence. Roper's 'heresy' causes More to prevent him from marrying Margaret, and in the scene where this topic is mentioned Roper lists some of the evils that were afflicting the Church at the time and which caused him to become a heretic – for a while. Note however, that More always made the distinction between the corruption of men who *ran* the Church, and the *teachings* of the Church.

More was a staunch Catholic and defender of the Roman Catholic Church. Like all Catholics, he believed that the Bishop of Rome, the pope, was a direct descendant of Peter, Christ's disciple. Note that 'descended' is used here in the sense of a direct and unbroken line of election and authority, passed on through one pope to the next. Each pope has traditionally been the Bishop of Rome. You do not have to agree with that view of the origin of a pope's authority, but you do need to accept that it was More's belief, if you are to grasp some of the reasons for the stand he takes against the King.

You also need to realize that through the centuries, popes have not only been the spiritual leaders of millions of people, but have also been earthly rulers, wielding power over their own country, and others. They have always had tremendous influence on world events and during the period in which the play has been set, most of the known Western world acknowledged the Pope as its spiritual leader.

In those days, marriage was one of the elements used for the strengthening of political ties between different countries. Under pressure from England and Spain the Pope, Clement VII, had made void a Christian law which forbade a man to marry his brother's widow, thus making it possible for Henry to marry Catherine. (Henry's brother, Arthur, to whom she had been married, had recently died.)

Henry had a daughter, Mary, by Catherine. (Mary eventually became England's first ruling queen.) However, Henry was afraid that if he had no son the Tudor line would end. Attracted to Anne Boleyn, and hoping she could give him the son he wanted, he asked the Pope to reverse the original decision so that he could declare his marriage with Catherine void and thus be able to marry Anne with a clear conscience. Clement VII refused and was supported in his decision by Spain. Perhaps his decision was also influenced by the fact that Spanish troops were occupying Rome at the time: they belonged to Emperor Charles V, who was Catherine's nephew.

After many negotiations and diplomatic delays, Henry declared himself the Supreme Head of the Church and the English clergy in 1531 'so far as the law of God allows'. The qualifying clause had been added by Bishop Fisher who was later to share More's fate. In 1532 the Convocation of Clergy agreed to submit to the King's will, and More resigned the Chancellorship. In 1533, Cranmer, the newly appointed Archbishop of Canterbury, annulled Henry's marriage to Catherine and claimed that his earlier, secret marriage to Anne Boleyn was valid.

More remained silent on the matter, but his absence from Anne Boleyn's coronation led to her enmity and a succession of charges were made against him. In 1534 Parliament passed the Act of Succession which made it necessary for all public figures to swear an oath acknowledging Anne Boleyn as Queen. On 13 April, Bishop Fisher and Thomas More refused to take the oath and were condemned to life imprisonment and forfeiture of their goods.

A new Act of Supremacy dropped Bishop Fisher's qualifying clause, 'so far as the law of God allows', and made it possible for the State to declare that anyone who denied the King his new titles would be guilty of treason. In the end it took an outrageous act of perjury by Rich to secure More's fate. More was executed on 6 July 1535. The Catholic Church beatified him on 29 December 1886. (Beatification is a declaration that the person had shown an 'heroic degree of holiness in his life'.) More was canonized (declared a saint) on 19 May 1935.

Anne Boleyn gave Henry a child, a daughter, Elizabeth. Elizabeth eventually became Queen of England, ousting her half-sister, Mary.

Summaries of themes

Conscience

More knew that his religious beliefs imposed upon him a duty to inform himself properly on those matters of importance in his life, and particularly so in respect of matters concerning conscience. In thus doing, once he had reached a decision as to the right course of action – known as having formed a 'certain conscience' – he must follow that conscience. To form a 'certain conscience' is no insubstantial matter and the decision is not arrived at lightly, but once arrived at it must be acknowledged and acted upon, unless compelling evidence to the contrary subsequently comes to light which would affect and change the original decision. More had formed such a 'certain conscience' on the matter of the King's marriage and was unable to ignore the duty this laid upon him without committing a serious sin.

Note that More does not suggest his conscience is necessarily true or right, but that 'what matters to me is . . . that I believe it to be true'. In believing something to be true, he must act accordingly.

Bribery
In an imperfect world it would seem that every man can be 'bought'. Minor examples of bribery exist in the play but the most spectacular, of course, is the acceptance of high office by Rich in return for perjured evidence against More. How well had Rich formed a 'certain conscience', or had he indeed ever bothered with his conscience? There is evidence early in the play that he had doubts about some of the actions he was taking, but his greed for power was too strong. It is interesting to look at the various characters to see how they justify their actions, and the importance they place on conscience; Cromwell's views are of particular note here. What sort of 'bribe' do Cromwell and Norfolk seek?

Sin
For More, the ultimate sin is to lose one's soul by compromise and concession to an imperfect world, to the extent that there is nothing left of one's individuality. The Common Man is a perfect symbol of this dilemma and is the opposite to More who makes a stand which ultimately leads to death. For More, however, death is infinitely preferable to the committing of sin, especially for mere earthly gain. Note, however, his refusal to judge the 'conscience' and therefore sinfulness of others. He reacts very strongly to Cranmer's suggestion that he could assess More's state of sinfulness.

There is no suggestion of Divine intervention in the affairs of Man or State in the play. Indeed, the author is at pains to indicate how the most corrupt and weak survive whilst the best die. Perhaps rewards and punishments for a good or evil life become due after death?

Self

Crucial to the central action of the play, the concept of 'self' is very closely tied to the concept of conscience. It is suggested that an individual is not just a cog in society's machinery, whether the machinery be that of a religion or the State. Whilst recognizing that man is a social animal and lives within a social system, he is also an individual, and it is this individuality that concerns us here. More puts this to Norfolk with the words 'Is there no single sinew in the midst of this that serves no appetite of Norfolk's but is, just, Norfolk?' There must be some 'benchmark' or 'touchstone' within any man by which he judges his own actions and achieves a dignity which marks him out from the lower animals. Is it perhaps a lack of such an awareness that allows men to become 'sheep' to be manipulated by others and respond, when accused of heinous crimes, with 'I only followed orders'?

More is suggesting that each man owes it to himself to establish such an awareness of self and to lead his life accordingly. Of course, one of the 'reasons' why man may not find such a self-awareness very attractive is that it carries with it the responsibility of being accountable for one's own actions. It is not an easy thing to stand by one's religious or political beliefs to the extent of sacrificing one's life for that belief. Those countless men and women through all ages who have, however, done so, whether Protestants, Catholics, Jews, Muslims, etc, or one of a hundred different political persuasions, ought to give us pause for thought.

Friendship/loyalty

It is interesting to follow the emphasis that so many of the characters place on the idea of friendship and loyalty, and the 'duties' they feel it imposes on them and their acquaintances. More has a healthy scepticism about the value of human friendship and given the actions of those around him it is an attitude that seems fairly well justified. Norfolk's plea to 'come with me, for fellowship' (note, if you ever use this quotation, he says 'fellowship' not 'friendship') basically makes an appeal which relies on a 'cosiness' and 'woolly' thinking which totally ignores personal dignity and self-awareness. It is an appeal to the sheep mentality which is so strong in man.

Family   More's love for his family is implicit. Throughout the play he shows intense concern for their welfare. He appears to have particularly strong love for his daughter Margaret and his loyalty to her and Alice and his concern for their welfare is obvious. Cromwell, in using them to try to subvert More from his course of action, was basically playing on strong family ties and loyalties. People with a conscience are not very comfortable people to have around. They make us aware of all sorts of obligations that we have and which we find it easier to ignore in the hope they may just go away. However, for those with a highly or even just well-developed conscience, the problem is even greater, especially when it brings them into conflict with those they love. But the true Christian ethic was never founded on the principle of taking the 'easy way out' for the sake of convenience, fellowship or even family.

State   Much of what has been said about the family applies to the State—a much more impersonal sort of 'family' but one which constantly makes demands on its members, demands which are as frequently backed by the threat of quite severe punishments. The loyalties owed to 'King and country' run deep in most societies, but, again, More would hold that man's loyalty to his own 'self' runs much deeper.

Imagery

In his preface to the play Bolt refers to his use of metaphors and poetic images. He uses water in all its aspects—rivers, currents, tides, navigation, etc—as a figure for the 'superhuman context' of More's life.

Bolt's proclaimed fondness for the use of metaphor makes it advisable to study his use of imagery. A particularly interesting section is that in Act 1 when Norfolk is describing an incident concerning falcons. The story can, of course, be taken at its face value, but in the light of the events of the whole play the import of the image of a 'royal' stooping hawk attacking a 'clever' heron is very clear. There are other images in the play which refer to animals; note for example, how the author combines images of animals with a reference to the Bible and a famous author in an attempt to insult Norfolk and break the 'bonds' of friendship.

Clothes   Clothes are used in the play as metaphors and symbols. The Common Man changes clothes with each role he plays. Rich's progression is indicated visually by the increasing richness of his garments. Wolsey's downfall is cleverly indicated by a discarded crimson garment being thrown unceremoniously into a basket.

Law

More was a trained lawyer and believed in the strength of the law to preserve justice. Note his angry rebuttal of Roper when it was suggested that he would 'cut down every law in England' to 'get after the Devil'. He clung to the legal maxim that 'silence gives consent' to protect himself from execution over his refusal to take the oath which would give legal justification to the setting aside of the marriage of Queen Catherine. It was only misuse of the law through perjury that eventually brought about his death.

Structure

The simple division of the play into two acts marks two great periods in More's life. In Act 1, we see his gradual promotion to a position of power, attained against a growing background of political and moral pressures: a period when, in various conversations, we begin to see the mettle of the man. The second act shows his gradual decline in power and the testing of his beliefs.

Against the rise and fall of More we can gradually chart the seemingly inevitable rise of Rich in wealth and influence, and not so obviously but ever present, the rise of Cromwell.

Do be aware of how the repetition of images (which has been previously discussed) sometimes far apart and at other times close together, gives a subtle continuity and strength to the play's development. For example, look at the image of 'mud' which affects the highest and the lowest in the land; near the end of Act 1, Henry 'proudly' holds out his shoe and says 'Look, mud' and near the end of Act 2, Alice tells the Jailer to take his 'muddy hand' off her. Within four pages of Act 2, Cromwell asks Norfolk, 'do you see some third alternative?' and Chapuys assures his Attendant, 'There's no third alternative'. On both occasions More is being discussed, and in each case the people concerned demonstrate their total lack of understanding with regard to More's motives and character.

Finally, do read carefully Robert Bolt's own preface to the play, as it is crucial to a full understanding of the author's intentions and meanings.

Analysis chart

Analysis chart

Important events	More suggests Rich is 'deteriorating'	More and Norfolk display unease over Cromwell	Cardinal Wolsey summons More to see him	More gives silver goblet to Rich	Wolsey attempts to persuade More to 'help him'	Cromwell and More meet	Chapuys questions More regarding Henry's divorce	More discusses Roper's wish to marry Margaret	Suggestion that More may be next Chancellor	Wolsey's death announced	Cromwell quizzes Rich over his friendship with More	Chapuys queries Cromwell's real role	More's steward an informant to Cromwell and Chapuys	Henry visits More	More warned not to interfere in Henry's affairs	Roper accuses More of studying his 'conscience'	More rejects Rich's plea for employment	More and Roper discuss law	Cromwell now Collector of Taxes for York	Rich questioned by Cromwell about the silver goblet	Cromwell burns Rich's hand
Act/scene	1.1				1.2	1.3		1.4		1.5				1.6					1.7		
Places																					
Richmond Palace					●																
Hampton Palace										●	●	●	●								
Hall of Westminster																					
More's house: Chelsea	●	●	●	●				●	●					●	●	●	●	●			
Thames' river bank						●	●														
Public house																			●	●	●
Tower of London																					
Characters																					
More	●				●			●		●				●					●		
Margaret	●							●						●							
Alice	●							●						●							
Roper								●						●							
Norfolk	●													●							
Cromwell	●					●				●									●		
Rich	●									●				●					●		
King	●				●									●							
Wolsey					●			●		●				●							
Chapuys										●											
Cranmer																					
Common Man	●				●					●											
Boatman						●															
Foreman																					
Headsman																					
Jailer																					
Matthew	●									●				●							
Publican																			●		
Themes																					
Conscience	●				●					●				●					●		
Friendship	●													●					●		
Imagery	●					●		●		●				●					●		
Law								●						●							
Self	●									●				●							
Structure	●					●				●									●		
Page in commentary on which scene first occurs	23				28	29		30		31				32					37		

Important events

	Chapuys again seeks More's support	More resigns his position as Chancellor	Cromwell tries to convince Norfolk that More is corrupt	Chapuys assumes More is on 'his side'	More refuses to accept letter from King Charles	More refuses to accept money for his writings	First inquisition of More	More quizzed about the 'Maid of Kent'	More attempts to end his friendship with Norfolk	Roper and Margaret tell More about a new Act of Parliament	Common Man relates the fate which befalls some characters	The Seventh Commission to enquire into More's case	More refuses to swear to the Act of Succession	Cromwell fails to persuade More to change his mind	More visited in jail by his family	Margaret fails to persuade More to change his mind	Trial of More	Announcement of Bishop Fisher's execution	Cromwell considers the meaning of silence	Rich commits perjury	Execution of More
Act/scene	2.1		2.2	2.3			2.4		2.5		2.6				2.7		2.8				2.9
Places Richmond Palace																					
Hampton Palace			●					●	●												
Hall of Westminster																	●	●	●	●	
More's house: Chelsea	●	●		●	●	●															
Thames' river bank									●	●											
Public house																					
Tower of London											●	●	●	●	●	●					●
Characters More	●		●	●			●		●		●				●		●				●
Margaret	●														●						●
Alice	●			●											●						
Roper	●														●		●				
Norfolk	●		●						●		●				●		●				●
Cromwell	●		●	●			●				●				●		●				●
Rich			●				●				●						●				
King	●		●	●			●								●		●				
Wolsey																					
Chapuys	●			●																	●
Cranmer											●										●
Common Man	●																●				
Boatman									●												
Foreman																	●				
Headsman																					●
Jailer												●			●						
Matthew	●		●																		
Publican																					
Themes Conscience	●		●	●			●		●		●						●				
Friendship	●		●	●			●		●		●						●				●
Imagery	●		●				●		●		●				●		●				
Law	●		●	●			●		●		●						●				●
Self	●			●							●				●		●				
Structure	●		●	●							●				●		●				●
Page in commentary on which scene first occurs	40		44	46			48		50		52				55		57				61

Finding your way around the commentary

Each page of the commentary gives the following information:

1 A quotation from the part of the play on which a comment is made, so that you can easily locate the right place in your text.

2 A series of comments, explaining, interpreting, and drawing your attention to important incidents, characters and aspects of the text.

3 For each comment, headings to indicate the important characters, themes, and ideas dealt with in the comment.

4 For each heading, a note of the comment numbers in this guide where the previous or next comment dealing with that heading occurred.

Thus you can use this commentary section in a number of ways.

1 Turn to that part of the commentary dealing with the scene you are perhaps revising for a class discussion or essay. Read through the comments in sequence, referring all the time to the text, which you should have open before you. The comments will direct your attention to all the important things of which you should take note.

2 Take a single character or topic from the list on page 20. Note the comment number next to it. Turn to that comment in this guide, where you will find the first of a number of comments on your chosen topic. Study it, and the appropriate part of your text to which it will direct you. Note the comment number in this guide where the next comment for your topic occurs and turn to it when you are ready. Thus, you can follow one topic right through your text. If you have an essay to write on a particular character or theme just follow the path through this guide and you will soon find everything you need to know!

3 A number of relevant relationships between characters and topics are listed on page 21. To follow these relationships throughout your text, turn to the comment indicated. As the previous and next comment are printed at the side of each page in the commentary, it is a simple matter to flick through the pages to find the previous or next occurrence of the relationship in which you are interested.

For example, you want to examine in depth the theme of conscience in the play. Turning to the single topic list, you will find that this theme first occurs in comment 5. On turning to comment 5 you will discover a zero (0) in the place of the previous reference (because this is the first time that it has occurred) and the number 7 for the next reference. You now turn to comment 7 and find that the previous comment number is 5 (from where you have just been looking) and that the next reference is to comment 11, and so on throughout the text.

You also wish to trace the relationship between More and Alice throughout the play. From the relationships list, you are directed to comment 28. This is the first time that both More and Alice are discussed together and you will now discover that two different comment numbers are given for the subject under examination – numbers 31 and 49. This is because each character is traced separately as well as together and you will have to continue tracing them separately until you finally come to comment 49 – the next occasion on which both More and Alice are discussed.

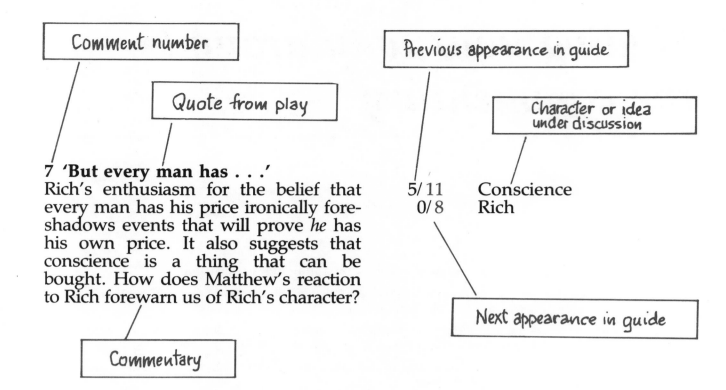

Comment number

Quote from play

Previous appearance in guide

Character or idea under discussion

7 'But every man has . . .'
Rich's enthusiasm for the belief that every man has his price ironically foreshadows events that will prove *he* has his own price. It also suggests that conscience is a thing that can be bought. How does Matthew's reaction to Rich forewarn us of Rich's character?

5/11   Conscience
0/8   Rich

Next appearance in guide

Commentary

Single topics:

Comment no:

Conscience	5
Friendship	13
Imagery	19
Law	46
Self	1
Structure	6
More	3
Margaret	16
Alice	16
Roper	46
Norfolk	13
Cromwell	10
Rich	7
King	18
Wolsey	36
Chapuys	56
Cranmer	214
Common Man	1
Boatman	43
Foreman	252
Headsman	239
Jailer	206
Matthew	6
Publican	99

Relationships:

			Comment no:
More	and	Alice	28
	and	Chapuys	57
	and	Cranmer	284
	and	Cromwell	10
	and	King	22
	and	Margaret	24
	and	Norfolk	13
	and	Rich	8
	and	Wolsey	36
	and	Conscience	5
	and	Friendship	13
	and	Law	46
	and	Self	3
Roper	and	Law	46
	and	Conscience	84
Cromwell	and	Rich	10
	and	Conscience	218
	and	Law	55
	and	King	187
Rich	and	Conscience	11
King	and	Conscience	39
	and	Law	121
Norfolk	and	Friendship	13
	and	Conscience	17

Commentary

Act 1, scene 1

1 *When the curtain . . .*
The opening stage directions give the audience a clear indication of the importance of the Common Man. Shortly, he will mention the 'Kings and Cardinals . . . and intellectuals', but in the basket of props we have a concrete image of all the other players on the stage of life, players who, to some extent, will find their expression through the words of the Common Man. However, do also be aware that the ease with which the Common Man changes identities does suggest a certain lack of self-identity, in striking contrast to More, 'the man for all seasons'.

2 *'It is perverse!'*
Does the suggestion that King or Cardinal would have had the 'right materials' and that an intellectual would have similarly 'coloured materials' indicate that the underlying themes of this play have more to do with matters of greater importance than the external appearances of King, Cardinal or intellectual? Would you agree that the references to 'speaking costumes' and 'embroidered mouths' could be considered as derogatory and provide a warning to the audience about what they might expect from such sources?

3 *'Is this a costume?'*
The references to the Common Man's costume, or virtual lack of it, and to 'Old Adam', should remind the audience of man's fall from grace in the Garden of Eden, where Adam learnt that he could not serve two masters: God and the Devil. The relevance of this will be seen later when we learn of the conflicts of conscience that More has to resolve for himself. This brief, physical self-examination by the Common Man foreshadows the much more detailed and crucial examination of 'self' which More will undertake and which other characters fail to undertake, or match up to.

4 *'Well, for a proposition . . .'*
In most theatrical experiences the audience is usually expected to 'suspend reality'—though not critical awareness—for a while and live the play as it unfolds before them; the mental suspension of present time and place giving its own sense of reality to the stage presentation. However, the Common Man's addresses to the audience and his act of actually donning a costume on stage tends, slightly, to 'divorce' the audience from the action, forcing them to adopt a more objective attitude to events as they unfold.

5 *'All right! A Common Man!'*
Matthew's proposition 'the Century of . . . other centuries' suggests that great 'figures' may strut about a national or international stage but that, ultimately, history is about the common man—about all of us. There is an association here with the idea implicit in the title of the play *A Man for All*

Characters and ideas previous/next comment	
0/2	Common Man
0/3	Self
1/3	Common Man
2/4	Common Man
0/5	More
1/5	Self
3/5	Common Man
4/35	Common Man
0/7	Conscience
3/6	More
3/8	Self

Seasons; More is the 'man for all seasons', and as such he provides a contrasting image to the 'common man', who in this play is seen as someone whose identity changes as frequently as the scenes change. More's adherence to the dictates of his conscience in the face of all temptation holds a message for all men, both commoner and King, and, as the Common Man implies, throughout all centuries.

6 'Is it good?'

This short exchange between the Steward and More highlights the petty pilfering in which the Steward indulges; but note how the theft of wine from these silver goblets will find its reflection in a much larger theme when More is later accused of perverting justice by taking bribes, in the form of a silver goblet. Just as here, that accusation will also be accompanied by lies and deceit. We also see here a brief indication of the awareness that More has of others' weaknesses, and his charitable response to their crimes.

0/34	Matthew
5/8	More
0/11	Structure

7 'But every man has . . .'

Rich's enthusiasm for the belief that every man has his price ironically foreshadows events that will prove *he* has his own price. It also suggests that conscience is a thing that can be bought. How does Matthew's reaction to Rich forewarn us of Rich's character?

5/11	Conscience
0/8	Rich

8 'Buy a man with suffering?'

Something of the way More's mind works can be seen in the way he interprets Rich's remark as suggesting that perhaps martyrdom, or dying for one's beliefs, could be attractive. Irony occurs here because this is exactly what happens to More – although he does not accept his fate because he finds the idea attractive! Rich is actually suggesting that suffering, in the form of torturing a person, is a way of discovering a man's price.

6/9	More
7/9	Rich
5/15	Self

9 'Oh. For a moment . . .'

Matthew's reaction to Rich finds some support in More's comment. More obviously did not expect anything profound from a conversation with Rich!

8/10	More
8/10	Rich

10 '. . . who recommended you . . .'

More correctly identifies the literary source of Rich's ideas, and as swiftly realizes that Rich has probably been 'pointed' in that direction by some other, more able, person. This fact is admitted by Rich, and the disclosure of Cromwell as the person tells us a great deal about Cromwell. Why does it? Could you imagine More, who was obviously familiar with the writings of Machiavelli, suggesting that Rich, an easily influenced character, should read them? More's comment that Cromwell is an 'able man' prefaced by an exclamation 'Oh . . .' suggests that More is not too enamoured by Cromwell.

0/25	Cromwell
9/12	More
9/11	Rich

11 'And he will do something . . .'

The irony of Rich shortly before commenting that every man has his price and now admitting he expects favours from Cromwell, ought to warn us that Rich almost certainly has 'his price', and prepares the reader for events to come later in the play.

10/12	Rich
7/12	Conscience
6/14	Structure

12 'Pardon me, Sir Thomas, . . .'

Would you agree that More 'knows' Rich in much more depth than Rich

11/13	Rich

thinks he has revealed about himself – in terms of the man's potential lack of conscience and moral fibre, and his greed for promotion and its accompanying power? To what extent does Rich know his own 'self', or does the drive to acquire wealth and power act as a barrier to the acquisition or realization of such knowledge? Certainly the account he gives of the months spent waiting for the opportunity to seek the favour of Cardinal Wolsey (then one of the most powerful men in Europe) suggests that Rich is obviously aiming high.

10/13	More
11/14	Conscience

13 'Oh, everyone's affable . . .'

In this brief reference to the distinction between 'friendship' and 'acquaintance' we see how Rich probably views his own relationship with More. We should also note that More counts the Duke of Norfolk as a friend. More obviously makes a clear distinction between his acquaintance with Rich, and his friendship with Norfolk!

0/29	Friendship
12/14	Rich
12/15	More
0/17	Norfolk

14 'What? What post?'

Rich's disappointed reaction to the news that the post is 'At the new school' leads on directly to the incident with the silver goblet. Note how this conversation with Rich, which started with talk of 'price' and ambition, ends with the same topic. But More gives Rich an object lesson in honesty, a lesson that Rich will singularly fail to learn; later in the play he will use this same goblet to demonstrate his own dishonesty and corruption.

12/17	Conscience
13/15	Rich
11/16	Structure

15 'And if I was who . . .'

More's response to Rich's question touches on the essence of self-knowledge. He feels that if Rich knew himself to be a great teacher, a knowledge shared by pupils, friends and God, this should be sufficient. A sense of peace and a quiet life follow from personal fulfilment, not from material ambition that puts a price on any man's conscience; 'speaking costumes' and 'embroidered mouths' do not signify that a man is at peace with himself and God. Rich is unable to believe that More seeks just peace and quiet, and that the office and influence he holds is not of his choosing. Note how during the course of this conversation the stage directions reflect More's growing unhappiness at Rich's attitude; from the 'gentle impatience' at the start they progress to 'grimly' for his last admonition 'Be a teacher'.

13/17	More
14/20	Rich
8/53	Self

16 'The Duke of Norfolk.'

Do Matthew's 'soapy' introductions, aimed at the audience, serve to reduce him further in our estimation, as well as letting us know who the new people are?

0/18	Alice
0/24	Margaret
14/42	Structure

17 'Well, damn my soul!'

This is a rather prophetic exclamation from Norfolk. It foreshadows the conversation he will have with More much later in the play. Can you identify when?

14/19	Conscience
15/19	More
13/18	Norfolk

18 'Matthew, get about . . .'

Alice's sharp remark to Matthew gives an indication of how she views him. Note that this conversation about hunting, whilst serving to let us get to know these new characters a little, also acts as an image for the conflict between More and Henry, and reflects the theme of water which permeates the entire play.

16/28	Alice
0/20	King
17/19	Norfolk

	Characters and ideas previous/next comment

19 'You see, Alice – . . .'

The image of the falcon, plummeting from the sky and ignoring all possible obstacles in its determination to catch the heron, reflects much of the ruthless determination of Henry in pursuing his own course of action. There is also a sense in which it reflects More in his single-minded determination to follow the dictates of his conscience, though his is a thinking, carefully considered path with much more than his life at stake. You need to be aware as you read this play that for More to embark on an action that would grievously offend God, and therefore lose his immortal soul, is a far more perilous course than any earthly threat might pose.

18/20	Norfolk
17/22	More
17/36	Conscience
0/20	Imagery

20 'The opinion of Aristotle . . .'

For the moment, Rich's contribution to the conversation is totally ignored. The reference just previously to 'an Act of God' and in the next few lines to 'a royal stoop' are interesting. If we associate Henry with the falcon you might bear these comments in mind when he later discusses his marriage with More. Then, he refers to his actions being in accord with God's will, reflecting Norfolk's 'Act of God' here. Equally, the 'royal stoop' could obviously be applied to Henry, the King of England. These references also hint at the loyalties and admiration that Norfolk has for the king.

You might like to consider another interpretation of the word 'stoop'. How low does Henry 'stoop' in his subsequent dealings with More and in his personal life? Wolsey made a critical reference in this regard when he talked about the King playing 'in the muck'.

19/21	Imagery
18/22	King
19/22	Norfolk
15/23	Rich

21 'The opinion of Aristotle . . .'

In this conversation we have the introduction of an important theme, that of water. Note carefully how its symbolism recurs throughout the play and especially in contrast with the dry land. Here, the mist obscures the passage of the falcon from its intended victim, and perhaps suggests the veil of lies and deceit that will surround the royal attack on More.

20/30	Imagery

22 'Oh, the *heron* was . . .'

The remark that the heron's action was 'discreditable' suggests the underlying attitude of Norfolk to 'clever' actions. It will be interesting to see if this attitude is reflected in Norfolk's reaction to More's defence of his own actions later in Act 2.

20/29	King
19/24	More
20/23	Norfolk

23 'I've never found . . .'

Norfolk's references to Aristotle, 'Great philosophy . . . Wonderful mind', strike the reader that he obviously has not read Aristotle's works, as indeed his comment on Machiavelli would tend to confirm. Would you agree that he is not a 'thinking' man as More will be shown to be? Rich's comment on the doctrines of Machiavelli, a few lines on, again shows him being effectively ignored – until he mentions Cromwell.

22/32	Norfolk
20/26	Rich

24 'You read it?'

The glance between More and his daughter Margaret indicates a shared amusement at Norfolk's attitude to women. It is also indicative of the close relationship they have – one which will be a crucial aspect of scenes later in the play.

16/33	Margaret
22/26	More

25 'You know Cromwell?'
The reaction to Rich's admission of knowing Cromwell, and Norfolk's news that Cromwell is now the Cardinal's secretary, seems to be greeted with some unease. Their reactions suggest that Cromwell is a man of whom to be wary, if not to fear.

10/43	Cromwell

26 'Do you *like* . . .'
The news that Rich likes Cromwell pleases More. It would seem that his conversation with him and the incident of the silver goblet have confirmed him in a dislike of Rich's attitudes, and he is relieved not to feel pressured to help the man attain a position in society which More feels would be unsuitable for such a weak character.

Elsewhere in the guide we comment upon the distinction More made between the corruption of men who ran the Church, and its teachings. Does More dislike Rich? Look at the comments he makes to Rich during the trial scene. What do they say about his attitude? It is valuable to try to assess More's reactions to the people around him, particularly in his conversations with Cromwell, Norfolk and the King.

23/27	Rich
24/27	More

27 'Sir Thomas, if only . . .'
Rich obviously has a great admiration for More, though whether that admiration stems from the power and prestige he has, or for his qualities as a man of conscience and intellect is not clear. Perhaps Rich is not sure himself! He has just admitted he 'likes' Cromwell, yet metaphorically, throws himself at More's feet. It suggests a man who will allow himself to be 'blown' by the latest wind, someone with a serious defect in his character.

26/28	More
26/31	Rich

28 'Talk of the Cardinal's . . .'
The summoning of More late at night, the reference to 'the King's business' followed by Alice's obscure reference to 'the Queen's business', quickly builds up the tension of the moment.

18/49	Alice
27/31	More

29 'Dear Lord give . . .'
The prayers of the More family are extremely ironic. The 'soul's salvation' is the very matter to which More and other characters will shortly have to address themselves, and perhaps the added blessing which More introduces is something to which Alice and Margaret would not have responded if they could have foreseen the events of the future!

13/82	Friendship
22/37	King

30 'No, down the river.'
The reintroduction of water imagery provides some interesting possibilities. Note how More is about to go upstream – a more difficult journey – to his interview with Wolsey which will be fraught with problems for him. Norfolk is about to embark on the easier journey, downstream, towards where the King is in residence.

21/42	Imagery

31 'Then good night!'
It is not a very helpful comment on More's part, but it is truthful. Rich's gratitude does nothing to lessen More's belief that Rich should be a teacher.

28/33	More
27/34	Rich

32 'Eh?' (*Delighted roar.*)
Norfolk's robust disrespect for the Cardinal gives us another pointer to the bluff nature of his character.

23/64   Norfolk

33 'Go to bed.'
The affectionate order should suggest to the reader a great deal about the relationship between More and his daughter. More knows that his daughter will probably wait up for him, and be concerned about the reason for this late summons.

31/34   More
24/48   Margaret

34 'Thank you, sir . . .'
Note how Rich has felt obliged to explain his possession of the goblet to Matthew. Can you imagine Norfolk doing so if the gift had been to him? Carefully note Matthew's comments about More: they crucially foreshadow the events to come; but subsequent events will show Matthew is not very accurate in his reading of More's character. His final comment that there must be something that 'he wants to keep' is correct. However, at this moment what 'it' is, is beyond Matthew's comprehension – is it beyond ours?

6/58   Matthew
33/36   More
31/54   Rich

Scene 2

35 'Thank you, sir . . .'
Note how Matthew changes the scene to Wolsey's palace before the audience's eyes, addressing them directly and thus distracting their attention from the scene-changing that is taking place.

5/51   Common Man

36 'Would you tell . . .'
There is an interesting insight here as to how Wolsey regards More, together with an insight into Wolsey himself. Perhaps you find it strange that a churchman of such high office suggests that taking a moral stance regarding 'facts' is of as much value as a 'squint'. Do bear in mind that in those days the Church was a powerful political as well as religious force, and its high officials did not necessarily get appointed because of their great piety!

19/39   Conscience
34/37   More
0/37   Wolsey

37 'Oh, spare me your . . .'
This contemptuous reference to Henry's affair with Anne Boleyn clearly indicates Wolsey's attitude to that relationship. However, it does nothing to lessen his determination to act on the King's behalf, to seek the solution the King wants for his lack of a son and heir.

29/39   King
36/38   More
36/38   Wolsey

38 'God's death, he . . .'
Wolsey seems amazed that More does actually pray to God for a resolution of Henry's problem – a wry comment on Wolsey's position as Cardinal. It was Alice who commented that Wolsey was a butcher's son and meant the reference to be derogatory. Do you think his comments here, 'That thing' (referring to Anne) and 'barren as a brick' (describing Catherine) justify her low opinion of him?

37/39   Wolsey
37/40   More

39 '–I think we might . . .'
We see here an indication of where Wolsey's loyalties seem to lie. Note that
he again returns to the theme of 'common sense' and 'statesmen'; he clearly
feels that 'conscience' is a matter which should not be allowed to interfere
with public life.

37/66	King
38/40	Wolsey
36/40	Conscience

40 'Let him die . . .'
Despite Wolsey's suggestion that the Church needs reformation he is still
prepared to make a further mockery of its values by manipulating it to the
State's benefit. In asking More how he can put his private conscience before
his duty to the State, he raises the central question which relates to the
essence of man's existence within a social context, not just then, but for all
time: to what extent is the State's claim on a man's loyalty and conscience all-
embracing? And in this context, does it supersede man's loyalty to God?
More's answer is not one that Wolsey wants to hear and he responds by
suggesting that prayers will not deal with his paperwork; but then, was
More actually suggesting that prayers would?

39/53	Conscience
39/41	Wolsey
38/41	More

41 'Like yourself, Your Grace?'
Wolsey's suggestion that More should become a priest as he is not worldly
enough for political life is shrewdly turned back on him by More. Wolsey is a
very worldly cleric indeed!

40/44	More
40/50	Wolsey

Scene 3

42 'Bless you, sir– . . .'
The reintroduction of the Common Man as a boatman marks the change of
scene. No doubt he saw More as a person from whom he could extract a
higher fare; however, the sudden appearance of Cromwell puts paid to this
idea. Given the geographical placings of the various residences, it is not
surprising that the river is used as a main highway, even without taking into
account the perilous state of any available roads! The river, however, is also
closely connected with the ebb and flow of More's fortunes; it will be much
further down the river, in the Tower of London, that More will eventually be
put to his final test.

30/45	Imagery
16/53	Structure

43 'Then you know . . .'
Cromwell's first words are to remind the Boatman of the legal conditions of
his licence, giving a small indication of the way his mind works. You might
also like to consider the use of the word 'fixed', by Cromwell. Look out for its
use by Cromwell later in the play and bear in mind its various meanings! We
have recently learnt that he had been appointed Wolsey's secretary but he
was not at the meeting with More. His sudden appearance would suggest
that he is interested in trying to discover what happened there.

0/193	Boatman
25/54	Cromwell

44 'Sir Thomas More!'
Just as with Cromwell, it is presumably no coincidence that Chapuys should
just happen to come across More at this time. As ambassador from Spain, a
Catholic country, he is concerned that no insult should be offered to Henry's
Spanish wife. Note the probing questions and the easy way in which More
turns them away. Chapuys' final comment, 'a nod is . . .' indicates that he
has taken away a very different idea of More's conversation with Wolsey

41/45	More

than actually happened. Do note how, in these two fairly brief conversations, More demonstrates how carefully he responds to probing questions—he will be given more cause to practise this skill later in the play.

45 'I'll pay what . . .'

More remarks that the river appears to be 'silting up', that is, clogged and muddied. It is an apt image for how his life is suddenly changing; he has just displeased two very powerful men who are obviously determined to embroil him in dangerous affairs of State. This 'muddying' of the river appears threatening, with the 'deep channel' becoming ever more narrow: as will be the way which More will find himself constrained to follow.

42/50	Imagery
44/46	More

Scene 4

46 'Sir Thomas, I'm . . .'

More is delighted that Roper has been accepted into the law profession. He obviously feels that it is an honourable calling; we shall see at a later stage if his faith in that calling is justified.

0/48	Law
45/47	More
0/47	Roper

47 'As long as he's . . .'

It's a little ironic that More should express a mild criticism of Roper's 'terribly strong principles'—it's similar to the accusation levelled at More by Wolsey not that long ago! Roper's sympathy with the Protestants is sufficient reason for More to refuse permission for him to marry Margaret. More importantly, the discussion provides the opportunity to introduce the matter of Henry requiring a divorce, a matter which so far no one has mentioned by name. Note that More indicates a liking for Roper, despite disagreeing with his beliefs. You might like to consider the differences between the characters of Roper and Rich, both of whom want something from More, but who go about their quests in very different ways.

46/48	More
46/84	Roper

48 'Mm? You know I . . .'

More deliberately ignores Margaret's question and then, when she persists, quite firmly rebuffs her interest. A few lines on he does exactly the same with his wife. One can understand his refusal to discuss the matter with Cromwell and Chapuys, but do you feel he is being over-cautious by refusing to discuss it with his own wife and daughter?

46/55	Law
47/49	More
33/64	Margaret

49 'Ah! Margaret—hot water.'

Note how quickly Alice's anger at Margaret for receiving Roper so late at night turns to concern for More when he sneezes. Her concern for his physical well-being is something that will cause More a great deal of worry later in the play. It is a pointer to her character which you should bear in mind.

48/50	More
28/64	Alice

50 'If Wolsey fell, . . .'

More's graphic account of the effects of Wolsey's fall will soon find its fulfilment. Note how he uses an image of boats and water.

45/51	Imagery
49/52	More
41/52	Wolsey

Scene 5

51 *The light is dimmed . . .*
Coming so swiftly after More's words, the dramatic action of a red cloak being thrown on the stage, closely followed by a cardinal's red hat, lets the audience know that events are moving swiftly. The unceremonious way in which the Common Man bundles the robes into his prop basket suggests scant respect for the office and dignity of Cardinal, and perhaps quite reasonably so, bearing in mind our short acquaintance with Wolsey.

52 ' "England's next Lord . . ." '
It is ironic that despite Wolsey's attempts to please the King, he dies en route to the Tower of London on a charge of treason. More has become Chancellor – why do you think he accepted? (You might like to look back at his conversation with Wolsey if you cannot think of the answer.)

53 ' "England's next Lord . . ." '
Yet again the Common Man offers a comment on More's character. Note how his words pick up the earlier conversation with Rich about 'suffering' and 'martyrdom'. (Sir Thomas does eventually become 'Saint Thomas', he was canonized by the Church in 1935.) However, does More's sainthood derive from his wilful 'indifference to realities' or from a clear perception of what the actual realities are? The awareness of one's true 'self' and 'conscience', and the obligations implied by that awareness are anything but 'indifference to realities', rather, they are the very opposite.

54 'Oh. Well, that's something.'
Cromwell makes Rich feel ashamed of his lowly job as librarian to Norfolk, who probably never reads a book. Note how he then goes on to talk of More, whom Rich denies was his friend. Rich is strictly accurate here, in the sense that More would not refer indiscriminately to anybody he knew as a 'friend', but his denial is much more associated with a desire not to lose Cromwell's favour – if he has it – or the chance of it, by acknowledging that he was associated with More. There is, perhaps, a biblical parallel here as when Peter denied he knew Christ, but Rich will eventually act out a far more treacherous role than one of mere denial. Note how throughout this scene there is a feeling of intrigue and deception, with each of the characters trying to probe and gain advantage from their acquaintances.

55 'Oh, *they* are the . . .'
Cromwell's cynicism about the value of Justices, Chancellors and Admirals – the English constitution – is a forewarning of the value he puts on justice and the rule of law. Are we left in any doubt of the work he does for Henry?

56 'Alas, Master Cromwell, . . .'
Chapuys' detailed knowledge about 'Great Harry' and of Henry's movements does not please Cromwell. It is obvious from their subsequent exchange about More that they both expect a different answer from him with regard to the matter of the divorce. To an extent their comments highlight the conflict they see between Church and State, but the mistake they both make is in seeing it as a conflict of political loyalties. Neither of them take into account the loyalty a man should have to his own conscience. Indeed, in religious terms it is, at the very least, not just a simple 'loyalty' one has to one's conscience but a compelling duty to obey it.

Characters and ideas previous/next comment

35/52	Common Man
50/62	Imagery
51/63	Common Man
50/53	More
50/71	Wolsey
52/118	Common Man
52/57	More
15/60	Self
42/58	Structure
40/57	Conscience
43/55	Cromwell
34/61	Rich
54/56	Cromwell
48/85	Law
55/57	Cromwell
0/57	Chapuys

57 'Sir Thomas is a man.'
Cromwell has a fairly limited vision of his fellow human beings. For someone who is obviously well read, it is surprising that he cannot conceive a situation where a 'man' may comprise much more than basic impulses of fear, greed, etc, as his answer would seem to imply.

53/64	More
56/58	Chapuys
56/58	Cromwell
53/73	Conscience

58 'Sir, Sir Thomas doesn't . . .'
There is an element of farce about this scene, with Chapuys and his attendant clearly hiding behind a nearby screen, Matthew's coy references to 'it', and the way he persuades Cromwell to make payment by embroidering More's reaction to the mention of the divorce. Can we believe Matthew's account? Despite only saying 'it', the Steward is obviously referring to the fact that More does not discuss the matter of the divorce with Alice or Margaret; we see now how wise he was in his reaction to their questions when he returned from the visit to Wolsey. Note the little structural links which occur: Matthew took a payment 'in kind' (the wine); the Boatman looked for extra payment; Matthew is again gaining extra payments from all and sundry; note the other occasions when the Common Man looks for additional payments in the play.

34/59	Matthew
53/62	Structure
57/59	Cromwell
57/59	Chapuys

59 'Sir Thomas rises at . . .'
Matthew gives Chapuys exactly what he wants to hear, that Sir Thomas is a devout Catholic. Chapuys, of course, interprets this as meaning that More will actively support his views and openly oppose the divorce. But he sees this only from a political perspective and not the position of conscience from which More views it.

58/61	Cromwell
58/60	Chapuys
58/60	Matthew

60 'No man can serve . . .'
You will recall the mention of Adam and the Devil near the start of the play; Chapuys now restates the idea in lucid terms. Does he really include God as one of the masters? Which master does the Common Man serve?

59/123	Chapuys
59/62	Matthew
53/81	Self

61 'What did he say?'
Is this conversation the first piece of evidence we have that Rich is now working for Cromwell?

59/99	Cromwell
54/87	Rich

62 'The great thing's . . .'
The Common Man reintroduces the imagery associated with water, and, particularly, the river. You will recall how the Common Man in his various guises is fairly avaricious. He is also very aware of the danger he is in from these great people, but equally is convinced that he can escape when the danger is too 'deep', by going 'deaf, blind and dumb'. You might look out for the next occasion he demonstrates an awareness of when he needs to become 'deaf, blind and dumb'.

51/63	Imagery
60/88	Matthew
58/99	Structure

Scene 6

63 *On this; a fanfare . . .*
The stage directions provide a feast of symbolism. The 'glittering blue light' reminds us of the water imagery with all its implied dangers; the fanfare

62/65	Imagery

speaks of the arrival of the King and the affairs of State for which he will look to More for help in solving; the plainsong, religious music, reminds us of the deeply religious nature of More. The stage is set for conflict.

64 'No sign of him, . . .'
The frantic search for More and his eventual appearance, simply dressed and explaining that he 'goes to Vespers' (that is, the saying of prayers at a particular time) highlights the huge difference there is between More's view of the situation and that of Alice, Margaret and Norfolk.

49/80	Alice
48/67	Margaret
57/65	More
32/68	Norfolk

65 'The service of God . . .'
Everybody has dressed with special care to meet the King except More, who refers to himself as a 'dowdy bird'. You might remember here the story of the falcon and the heron: the heron survived to return to its chicks – will More?

63/66	Imagery
64/69	More

66 Henry, *in a cloth* . . .
We have a resplendent picture of Henry in a cloth of gold descending 'slowly to their level'. You must remember that in More's time the king had absolute power. He was viewed as having been appointed king by God, and his word, on earth, was law. Note the immediate introduction of the opposing images of land and river. Henry refers to 'my river', but the picture of him with mud on his shoes suggests that, in contrast, the certainties represented by the land have been 'muddied'. There seems to be a clear distinction here between the river on which Henry travels and the firm land which More occupies.

65/76	Imagery
39/67	King

67 'Among women I pass . . .'
Margaret's first answer to Henry shows wit and appropriate modesty. She then displeases him with a display of Latin knowledge greater than his. How does she make it up to him? Do be aware of how important it seems to be to keep the King in good temper; note how More holds his daughter into her curtsey, making sure she is still there when the King turns.

66/68	King
64/68	Margaret

68 'Well, *I* dance . . .'
The King's abrasive vitality is amusing but dangerous. Note that he is ready to throw Norfolk to the ground just to show off to Margaret. Norfolk, whilst concerned for his dignity, is obviously aware that, if put to it, he will have to allow himself to be thrown.

64/128	Norfolk
67/69	King
67/69	Margaret

69 'Yes, Your Grace, I –'
Margaret's signal on a whistle is the cue for the King to display a full band of musicians who travel with him. It is his own music they are playing. Note how everyone must bow to the King's ego. The display of royal power adds point to the dangerous nature of the conversation about to take place between the King and More, and highlights the depth of feeling that More must hold in order to take such a huge risk as to deny the King anything he wants.

68/70	King
68/131	Margaret
65/70	More

70 'No courtship, no ceremony, . . .'
More does not answer the King when he is asked whether he is a friend. Can one ever be a 'friend' to a King, especially in the sense that More would view

69/71	King
69/71	More

the word? Here, no doubt, More is conscious that being the King's friend
will probably entail rather more than he cares to contemplate.

71 'Was he? Was he so?'

The King's angry outbursts against Wolsey should serve as a clear warning
to More of what the King has in mind for him to do, and the probable
consequences of failure. Note the King changes topics before More can
reply. Is the King, for a moment, not sure how to approach the matter with
More?

70/72	King
70/72	More
52/0	Wolsey

72 'Touching this matter . . .'

Henry has obviously decided to approach the matter of the divorce in a
much more conciliatory tone than his opening words about Wolsey. It is
quite evident that he has a great deal of respect for More and his abilities.

71/73	King
71/73	More

73 'There is my right arm.'

More's 'practical proposition' briefly places Henry in an awkward dilemma.
He is well aware of More's honest nature and the reference to matters of
conscience causes him to pause for a moment. The fact that Henry admits he
has broken his word to More bodes ill for their future relationship.

57/74	Conscience
72/74	King
72/74	More

74 'Ha! So I break . . .'

The King attempts to justify the divorce by quoting the Bible, and brushes
aside More's reference to a conflicting passage. He is quite accurate when he
goes on to comment that a man doesn't need a Pope to 'tell him when he's
sinned'. What do you think weighs most heavily on his mind, the sin he says
that he has committed, or his strong wish to remarry, fired by his desire for a
male heir?

73/75	Conscience
73/75	King
73/75	More

75 'Because you are . . .'

Note the King's assessment of his fellow men; can you think of incidents in
the play which justify his low opinion of them? Would you make a
distinction between the reasons for Norfolk's and Cromwell's loyalty – are
they both as bad as each other?

74/76	Conscience
74/76	King
74/76	More

76 'No, Thomas, I respect . . .'

Henry uses the image of water in a desert to indicate the value of the respect
he holds for More. Would you agree that he wants More's support to placate
his own uneasy conscience?

75/84	Conscience
66/79	Imagery
75/77	King
75/77	More

77 'No opposition I say!'

Henry is obviously determined to go his own way on this matter and, having
failed to get More to go with him, warns him against any form of opposition.
His comments about the use of the Bible and the Bishop of Rome being
under threat are not terribly persuasive – one can imagine him adopting
exactly the same tactics if he had the opportunity!

76/78	King
76/78	More

78 'I have no Queen!'

Henry's declaration that all who continue to recognize Catherine as his wife
are traitors is the final warning. After this meeting with More we do not
meet Henry again in the play. The fact that he does not appear again, helps

77/79	King
77/79	More

to prevent the play from becoming merely the account of a conflict between two men and allows us to concentrate on the central question of 'self' and 'conscience'.

79 'Eight o'clock you said?'

The King makes the changing tide an excuse for not staying to dinner. To what extent do you think that More's inability to please him has led to a change in the 'tide' of More's fortunes? Note the emphasis here: 'tide' is mentioned four times in the next few lines. Is there a suggestion that he feels More is out of touch with reality when he says 'I have forgotten . . . time flows past outside'?

76/90	Imagery
78/121	King
78/81	More

80 'Be ruled! If you . . .'

Alice is not a politician, yet she senses the error of opposing the King. The pressures on More to change his mind will start growing from now on, and the most distressing of these will be from his family.

| 64/82 | Alice |

81 'I neither could nor . . .'

The 'little area' where More must rule himself is crucial to the understanding of his reasons for refusing to go along with what the King wants. He would be willing to give the King his body, as witness their conversation a little earlier, 'Take your dagger . . .', but there is a limit: his soul is not at the King's disposal. More will return to this theme later in the play when he has a dispute with Norfolk about how far one may go for 'friendship's sake'.

| 79/82 | More |
| 60/130 | Self |

82 'And *you* stand . . .'

Is Alice right here? Does More stand between Anne Boleyn and the King? In a sense he does, because he refuses to accede to the King's wishes and salve the King's conscience for him. More's next comment, however, is the more accurate. The Sacrament of Marriage, between Catherine and Henry, is what stands between Henry and Anne. Note how More interprets Alice's injunction to be 'friends with him'; is 'flattery' something we would associate with More?

80/83	Alice
29/102	Friendship
81/83	More

83 'Yes – we shall be . . .'

When More says he is 'not the stuff of which martyrs are made' is he reassuring himself or Alice? Would you agree that at this stage More is aware of how this matter might develop, and of the likely consequences for himself?

| 82/84 | More |
| 82/96 | Alice |

84 'Must everything be . . .'

Roper touches upon the matter of how inconvenient a conscience may be. He recognizes that man is ruled by something other than the pressures of material life; his concern about whether or not he should accept a seat in Parliament, and his condemnation of the 'body' of the Church suggests he has similar concerns to those of More. Note his reference to the 'body' of the Church, that is the men and women who are its members and who enforce its rule. He obviously sees a clear distinction between them and their wrongdoings, and the 'teachings' of the Church.

83/85	More
76/85	Conscience
47/85	Roper

85 'I don't stand . . .'

More is very aware, more so than others would give him credit for at times, that his office does place all sorts of serious duties on him. It will become

| 55/91 | Law |
| 84/86 | More |

	Characters and ideas previous/next comment

more obvious as the play develops just how much reliance More places on the law and the strict observance of it. Despite the genuine friendship he feels for Roper, his conscience would not allow him to lightly view treasonable statements. Roper, for all his conscience, has yet to appreciate fully the ramifications of being 'ruled by conscience'.

84/86   Roper
84/92   Conscience

86 'Sophistication. It is what . . .'
Roper is here accusing More of abandoning his principles. He is obviously woefully misinformed, but the accusation is one that can be applied to all ages and especially the 20th century, when being 'sophisticated' is all too easily advanced as a reason for abandoning any hint of *self*-discipline and reference to 'conscience'.

85/87   More
85/91   Roper

87 'You have heard of me?'
Rich has 'jumped the gun' in his assumption that his reputation has preceded him, and it suggests that he has some guilty secrets. More's awareness of Cromwell's activities ought to come as no surprise: his careful actions in the past have suggested that he knows he will be spied upon.

86/89   More
61/89   Rich

88 'I know it.'
In trying to slide away when Rich accuses him of being an informant Matthew actually draws attention to himself and effectively confirms the accusation. The audience is already aware of Matthew's disloyalty.

62/145   Matthew

89 'You look at me . . .'
One can imagine why More will not now employ Rich who is almost certainly in the pay of Cromwell, but is this the real reason? It is more likely that More still sees Rich for what he really is and recognizes that his salvation can come only through following the profession of teacher or something similar; morally he is too weak to be placed in a position of power.

87/90   More
87/90   Rich

90 'I'm adrift. Help me.'
Rich is very much 'adrift'; he is able to see that he ought to strike out for the safety of dry land through teaching. Instead, he is at the mercy of the river, being swept along by his greed for power.

89/91   More
89/102   Rich
79/91   Imagery

91 'There is no law . . .'
More refuses to abuse the law of the land for his own convenience. Note how a few lines on he uses the imagery of water to clarify his thoughts. He will not attempt to 'navigate' 'right and wrong', but the law is another matter. Note also how this imagery contrasts the certainties of the land, with the use of words such as 'thickets' and 'forester', against the uncertainties of water with its 'currents', 'eddies', and the need to 'navigate'. There is an irony in his faith in the law, as later the State will ensnare More and cause his downfall by abusing the law – something which More refuses to do here.

90/94   Imagery
90/92   More
86/92   Roper
85/92   Law

92 'Oh? And when the last . . .'
More's great trust in the law of the land can be seen here. More wants to avoid the 'currents and eddies of right and wrong' or the dangerous course (upon which Henry is embarked) of making moral decisions for political reasons. He is not, as accused by Roper, setting man's law above God's, but

85/112   Conscience
91/93   Law
91/93   More
91/93   Roper

he knows and can find his way through man's law, and in this he hopes to find safety for the beliefs which his conscience tells him he must follow.

---

93 'I have long suspected . . .'
The 'golden calf' was an idol created by the Israelites in the Old Testament; they worshipped it instead of God. Do you think there is a sense in which More has almost made the law *his* golden calf?

92/94	Law
92/95	More
92/98	Roper

---

94 'Are you sure . . .'
Once more the law is couched in imagery of dry land – thickets – whilst Roper's shifting beliefs are referred to as the 'mainmast of your sea-going principles'.

91/98	Imagery
93/97	Law

---

95 *Exit* More. *They all . . .*
More's abrupt exit indicates the growing stress he is under.

93/96	More

---

96 'He said nothing . . .'
Note Alice's flush of jealousy that More has not expressed direct concern for her. More has a very different relationship with Alice, compared to that with his daughter, Margaret. Do you think he regards Alice as being of less worth? Look closely at their conversations for evidence one way or another. What is it that he admires in Margaret, and in Alice?

83/130	Alice
95/97	More

---

97 'I stand on the wrong . . .'
More is correct: he breaks no law, but he has offended Henry – the most powerful man in the kingdom. As the law would have it, he is safer than any man in England; however, the distinction Roper made between the 'body' of the Church and its teachings may equally well be made between the law, as written, and the men who will manipulate it.

94/107	Law
96/98	More

---

98 'I'm a prominent figure.'
More considers that Roper's principles are as unstable as water when affected by violent weather. Would you agree with him?

94/104	Imagery
97/104	More
93/120	Roper

Scene 7

99 ' "The Loyal Subject" . . .'
The Common Man hangs an inn sign to set the scene. Note the irony in its title. Words like loyalty and friendship are so often used interchangeably and to convey a whole range of loaded implications. Note all those characters who attempt to use the loyalty and friendship of others, and to what purposes.

61/100	Cromwell
62/111	Structure
0/100	Publican

---

100 'Is this a *good* . . .'
The Publican puts into practice much of Matthew's determination to be 'deaf, blind and dumb', much to Cromwell's amusement. Note also how he takes his 'payment' to ensure he forgets his visitor.

99/101	Cromwell
99/0	Publican

	Characters and ideas previous/next comment

101 'The master statesman . . .'
What does Cromwell's assertion that kings are born 'drunk' with success reveal about his own character and ambition? Is he drunk with ambition, or very coldly and calculatingly ambitious? How would you justify your answer?

100/102 Cromwell

102 'Well, nothing said in . . .'
Rich declares he would never repeat words said in friendship. Do you believe him? Have we seen any evidence so far of how trustworthy Rich is?

101/103 Cromwell
82/103 Friendship
90/103 Rich

103 'It would depend . . .'
Cromwell forces Rich to concede that he could be bribed to betray a friend. Can you recall Rich's first conversation with More? There is a certain prophetic irony about that conversation which finds its fulfilment in this scene. Can you see why?

102/133 Friendship
102/104 Cromwell
102/104 Rich

104 'There are *some* things . . .'
How does this remark of Rich's match up with his earlier statement about every man having his 'price'? Is Rich ever put to the test on this matter? Do you think that More has one of the 'lifelines' to which Cromwell is referring? Presumably the 'lifeline' would be More's adherence to the dictates of his conscience, and his suggestion that he is not the 'stuff of which martyrs are made' might prompt us to think that perhaps he, too, hopes he will never have to test his 'lifeline'. Note the imagery of a 'lifeline' which links the land and water images.

98/118 Imagery
98/113 More
103/105 Rich
103/105 Cromwell

105 'I think you'd make . . .'
Rich is given office as Collector of Revenues in return for his 'services' to Cromwell. He has not, so far as we know, actually done anything to justify his reward. So why do you think he is being rewarded?

104/106 Cromwell
104/106 Rich

106 'Get sure.'
There is something rather humorous about this exchange on religion with Rich being 'Almost sure' he is not religious and Cromwell's sharp 'Get sure' in response. What is Cromwell afraid of here? Perhaps he has More in mind?

105/107 Cromwell
105/108 Rich

107 'Whose convenience?'
There is an echo of a recent conversation between More and Roper here, can you see where? The reintroduction of the matter of Henry's divorce refocuses our attention on the central issue.

106/108 Cromwell
97/119 Law

108 'You lost that some . . .'
More was afraid Rich would lose his innocence and his fears have been realized. Cromwell's ability to judge the quality of the man he is dealing with is sometimes as perceptive as More's (how well does he assess More?), but note the contemptuous way he refers to that lost innocence. You would do well to bear in mind the ruthlessness that Cromwell demonstrates here; it bodes ill for More's reliance on the 'thickets of the law'.

107/109 Cromwell
106/110 Rich

109 'Yes, I say he is.'
Despite Cromwell's obvious ability he seems unable to conceive that the

100/110 Cromwell

aura which surrounds the position of 'Pope' can be more than a 'meaning-less circumstance' which will prove to be what Rich calls an 'administrative inconvenience'. Is it that he is so corrupt himself in his search for more and more power that he is unable to accept that some men are not corrupt and are incorruptible?

---

110 'Just so. This goblet that . . .'
Cromwell doesn't actually need Rich to tell him anything about the goblet: it is obvious that he already knows all about it. However, in making him recount its history and More's involvement, Cromwell sets Rich on the first easy step towards the betrayal of More.

109/113   Cromwell
108/112   Rich

---

111 'Where did he . . .'
Remember how More was offered this goblet as a bribe? Now Cromwell is attempting to use it as a means of ensnaring More, and Rich, who benefited from More's generosity, will effectively throw the gift back in More's face. The silver goblet, which Rich so valued for what it could purchase him, turns out to have purchased the betrayal of the man he wanted to call 'friend'.

99/122   Structure

---

112 'There, that wasn't . . .'
The carefully planned corruption of Rich by Cromwell is proceeding quite smoothly. However, there is an irony in Cromwell's 'wasn't too painful' which Rich will soon discover! How accurate is Cromwell's judgment that Rich will find betraying his friend easier next time?

92/196   Conscience
110/116   Rich

---

113 'Well there *are* these . . .'
Note the contempt that Cromwell obviously feels for the 'upright' and 'steadfast' men. His analysis of these men suggests that they want to be the 'constant factor' in any situation. What do you think of his opinion? Does More want to upset Henry and place his life in jeopardy?

110/114   Cromwell
104/115   More

---

114 'If they've any sense . . .'
What 'sense' is Cromwell talking about here? Would it be right to suggest he is talking about a sense of self-preservation?

113/115   Cromwell

---

115 'What none at all?'
Cromwell's casual attitude towards religion a little earlier in this conver-sation finds a reflection in this remark. His priority obviously lies in this world; to him, Heaven is as unreal as a man who cannot be bribed. He knows More is a brilliant man, and he infers that brilliance automatically includes having the sense to preserve one's earthly body, at any cost. More, however, has different priorities–can you say what they are? More has already said he is 'not the stuff of which martyrs are made', now Cromwell suggests he *could* be frightened. Are they both wrong?

114/116   Cromwell
113/116   More

---

116 'Doesn't know how to . . .'
In burning Rich's hand Cromwell suggests the depths to which he is prepared to sink in order to make his point. There is an irony in his action as well. Remember Rich's interest in the idea of making a man suffer physically? He gets some firsthand experience of it here!

115/117   Cromwell
115/120   More
112/154   Rich

117 'You enjoyed that!'
What did Cromwell enjoy? Was it the act of physically hurting someone or the demonstration of his power over a lesser man? What assessment would you make of his character at this moment? Do remember his attitudes towards other men – More, Chapuys, the Common Man – as well as his treatment of Rich.

116/138   Cromwell

Act 2, scene 1

118 'The interval started . . .'
In commenting on the passage of time, the Common Man reintroduces the imagery of water. Note the many references; 'water . . . under the bridge', 'floating along', 'torrents', 'canals' etc. The promise for change that the river always represented has been fulfilled by the setting up of the Church of England. Do be aware that this play is not concerned with the historical arguments that surround the break between Rome and Henry. What it is concerned with is the conscience of one man, More. Why he acted as he did and the pressures that surrounded his actions are the central themes of the play.

53/119   Common Man
104/119   Imagery

119 'The interval started . . .'
The Common Man's comment about 'imprisonment without trial' and torture should not unduly surprise us. Such practices were not unknown. However, for men of the stature of More, things often took a little while longer, and we may assume he is one of the 'unhappy few'. Note the ironic tone of the whole of this passage with its 'torrents' of religious passion and the 'canals' of moderation.

118/249   Common Man
118/144   Imagery
107/121   Law

120 'My allegiance to . . .'
Roper's 'conversion' to the Church of Rome has remained firm since we last met him at More's house. More's comment about the treatment he would have received in Spain during his 'heretic period' gives some idea of the bigotry which attended the outward signs of religion in those days.

116/121   More
98/122   Roper

121 'Supreme Head of the . . .'
Henry has declared himself Supreme Head of the Church in England. Would you consider that More is splitting hairs here? Certainly such a legal 'quibble' is often so regarded by the layman. However, so far as More is concerned, the actual letter of the law may be all that stands between him and death. His attitude, therefore, must be that if he can take the protection offered by the law's 'thickets', then he will and must do so, if he is to protect his conscience and his body. It was the clause 'so far as the law of God allows' which provided an area in which More and others who opposed the Act could exercise their freedom of conscience.

119/126   Law
120/122   More
79/125   King

122 'Don't! If your opinion's . . .'
Roper is now married to Margaret. More urges him to be cautious of treasonable thoughts as this would endanger his family. You will recall how More, earlier in the play, was equally cautious of involving his wife and daughter in affairs of State that could have endangered their lives.

121/123   More
111/131   Structure
120/140   Roper

123 'May I not come simply, . . .'
More's close friend Erasmus, the scholar and theologian, likened More to the
Greek philosopher Socrates as they demonstrated similar clear thought on
ethics and politics. Socrates was eventually ordered by the State to poison
himself for 'misteaching' the youth of his country. Here, More is saying that
if Chapuys has come to suggest he enters into open conflict with Henry on
the matter of the divorce, he is wasting his time. What would make you
think that Chapuys is lying when he says he is coming simply to 'pay his
respects' to More?

60/124	Chapuys
122/124	More

124 'A characteristic we . . .'
Note that More is not impressed by Chapuys' 'we are brothers in Christ',
and quickly addresses him by his formal title to emphasize the nature of his
visit. More has no wish to be accused of secret meetings with the Spanish
Ambassador.

123/125	More
123/125	Chapuys

125 'Tisn't "holy", Your . . .'
An immediate effect of Henry's break from the Church in Rome was a
decline in the use of Latin in ecclesiastical matters. More is swift to correct
Chapuys, and prevents himself being drawn into any criticism of his King.

121/128	King
124/126	More
124/126	Chapuys

126 'My Lord, I cannot . . .'
Carefully note the sequence of Chapuys' argument over the next few lines,
and More's response. He is agitated by Chapuys' comments. Does he see
some justification in them? Do you? Does there come a point when a man
such as More, to whom so many look for guidance, has to cease trying to
shield himself behind the 'thickets of the law' and state his case plainly? Or
is More correct in suggesting that another man in his position might have
made things even worse for the Church? It is not an easy case to answer.
More's social, political and religious responsibilities to other men are all
subject to the responsibilities he feels to himself and his family. Which come
first? As More would have it, his 'self' must follow the dictates of his
'conscience'. His duty to his soul and to God are totally clear, but as to the
'currents and eddies' of what is right and wrong in respect of his duties to
other men, matters are not so clear.

112/135	Conscience
125/127	More
125/127	Chapuys
121/127	Law

127 'Believe me, my lord, . . .'
Chapuys is on the verge of inciting More to treason. Would you agree that
More will find this much easier to deal with than those comments Chapuys
was making a few moments earlier? From your knowledge of More's
character how did you think he was going to react to Chapuys here?

126/128	Chapuys
126/129	More
126/142	Law

128 'One moment, Roper, . . . '
Norfolk's instant hostility to the Catholic Chapuys indicates his loyalty to the
King. That his loyalty is total is seen in the language he uses, for example
'knuckled under'. Do you think his change of religious allegiance cost him
much searching of heart or conscience? What evidence was there before this
that he was the 'King's man'?

127/138	Chapuys
125/136	King
68/132	Norfolk

129 'It's quite unintentional.'
Note how even in this most distressing of moments for More he manages to
keep a sense of humour, deliberately interpreting Norfolk's remark about
Chapuys in a literal sense.

127/131	More

130 'Hell's fire – God's . . .'
The pressures on More to save himself, his earthly self, are now going to mount quite alarmingly. Look at the catalogue of things that Alice says he is betraying. She cannot believe, let alone understand, that anything can be put in balance with them and weigh more. It is crucial to understand More's position here. Put very simply, if a man has no respect for his 'self', then he is as nothing. There are, one hopes, for each of us bounds which it is inconceivable we should overstep; for each person they will be different. More has been brought face to face with his 'bounds'. One wonders where or whether Cromwell, Rich or Norfolk would draw a line.

96/131	Alice
81/134	Self

131 'If you want.'
We commented earlier on the differences in the relationship between More, Alice and Margaret. Margaret agrees to help him because she understands what he has to do. Ironically, the arguments that Chapuys was recently putting to him have now, to an extent, seen their outcome.

130/139	Alice
129/132	More
122/144	Structure
69/140	Margaret

132 'All right I will – . . .'
Norfolk's estimation of More's act is that it is cowardice. Why might it be seen in that light? Do you see his act as cowardice? Can you justify your opinion from evidence in the play? The separation of Church and State places those institutions in conflict. For More, the fact that the Pope may be a bad one does not alter the fact of the link with St Peter 'our only link with Christ'. Breaking that link, for him, must be wrong.

131/134	More
128/133	Norfolk

133 'Man, you're cautious.'
Norfolk does not understand More's principles, and feels angered by his cleverness. It has been mentioned before that he is not a learned man; he understands action, loyalty and friendship. Or does he? How would you describe Norfolk's view of loyalty and friendship? Don't forget to refer to the text of the play to support your views!

103/135	Friendship
132/135	Norfolk

134 'The Apostolic Succession . . .'
Read More's words very carefully. They reiterate the key to the thinking behind the decisions he has to take, and is taking.

132/135	More
130/169	Self

135 'Have I your word, . . .'
Does More 'lay traps' for Norfolk? Given our knowledge of Cromwell and his view of men, how well does More predict the times? Norfolk's comment about 'lawyer's tricks' is very apt. That is virtually all More has left to keep him safe!

126/149	Conscience
133/143	Friendship
134/137	More
133/137	Norfolk

136 'And here's your answer.'
Quite obviously the King had anticipated More's answer. Look back to his conversation with More and see whether you think the King will be satisfied to leave matters as they are.

128/151	King

137 'Oh, Howard!'
More passes on Chapuys' warning about the danger of insurrection in the North. In 1536 the North rebelled under the leadership of Robert Ashe in a movement called 'The Pilgrimage of Grace'. This was savagely put down by

135/139	More
135/148	Norfolk

the King. Note More's righteous anger at Norfolk's foolish jibe a few lines
on. What light does it throw on Norfolk's character?

138 'We will. We do . . .'
Should we have suspected that Cromwell would be keeping a close eye on
Chapuys? One can imagine what sort of 'hand' Cromwell has on matters!

128/169	Chapuys
117/144	Cromwell

139 'Not at all, . . .'
Alice's question has a great deal of bitterness about it. She feels somehow
betrayed by her husband but cannot understand why. More seems pleased
to look forward to retirement with his family – or is he? Why do you think
Alice doesn't want to learn to read? Is it because she associates such
'cleverness' with the actions of her husband, and does not want to be
tarnished in the same way?

131/141	Alice
137/140	More

140 'Sir, you've made . . .'
Would you agree that Roper still does not understand why More has acted in
the way he has? Do *you* understand? Margaret seems to suggest she
understands her father, but is not given the opportunity to expand her
answer.

131/233	Margaret
139/142	More
122/229	Roper

141 'Oh, you'd walk on the . . .'
Alice's 'uneducated' love for her family gives her a clearer understanding of
the huge danger More is in. Her instinct serves her better than anybody
suspects.

139/143	Alice

142 'If we govern our . . .'
More is going to take refuge in silence. Here he explains very simply the
stand he is going to take, and the importance of keeping to it.

140/143	More
127/144	Law

143 'Look – . . . I'm the Lord Chief . . .'
Note how closely this demonstration parallels the one he gave Norfolk a few
minutes before. More can quite clearly see that all his acquaintances and
family will be used in an attempt to 'snare' him. He is equally determined
that there shall be no way in which that can happen. He will protect them
from themselves, and in doing so, protect himself.

141/166	Alice
142/144	More
135/145	Friendship

144 'And so it must . . .'
More trusts the law as his shield from unjust attack. Note the link here,
almost word for word, with what Cromwell said to Rich in an earlier scene.
Do More and Cromwell use this image of a lifeline in slightly different ways,
and also view the circumstances of its likely use differently?

138/146	Cromwell
119/162	Imagery
143/145	More
131/157	Structure
142/153	Law

145 'What about you Matthew?'
The Steward's earthly cynicism about More's motives is both amusing and
sad. In imputing to More a desire to get his services at a reduced rate he
shows his own avaricious nature. Despite his closeness to the family he fails
to really 'know' them, especially More, because he is too bound up in his
own affairs. His loyalty starts and finishes with himself.

143/154	Friendship
88/157	Matthew
144/146	More

Scene 2

	Characters and ideas previous/next comment

146 'Not being a man of . . .'
You will recall how, all along, More has insisted on not commenting on Henry's marriage to Catherine. His silence is his only protection now, but according to Cromwell it 'is bellowing up and down Europe'. Quite obviously, 'Europe' is interpreting his silence as being a sign he is against Henry. Are they right? Be careful how you answer this. Has More's view on the matter yet been stated anywhere in the play?

144/147	Cromwell
145/153	More

147 'We may say then, . . .'
It is ironic that, like Europe, Cromwell is going to interpret More's actions, but this time to support Cromwell's view of More's intentions. On how many previous occasions has Cromwell effectively stated that More 'will line up on the right side'? Ironically, More might agree with him, but then More's perception of which is the 'right' side is likely to be different.

146/149	Cromwell

148 'Yes! Crank he may . . .'
What was Norfolk's opinion of More when we first met him, earlier in the play? Did he then think of More as a crank? What, then, has turned More into a 'crank'? Could it be that Norfolk's opinion of More's actions tells us more about Norfolk than it does about More?

137/150	Norfolk

149 'And with a little . . .'
Returning to his theme that all men are susceptible to corruption, Cromwell yet again demonstrates how little he knows More. It also demonstrates how casually he views the substance of the dispute, but not his determination to serve the King's wishes.

135/168	Conscience
147/152	Cromwell

150 'I still say let . . .'
Could it be that because Norfolk realizes it will not be so easy to change More's views that he wants to try (not very forcefully though) to protect his old friend? Certainly, the course he advocates here is the one that More wishes to follow.

148/151	Norfolk

151 'The King does not . . .'
Notice how quickly Norfolk abandons his suggestion to do nothing. The implied threat of the King's displeasure is sufficient. Norfolk obviously has a well-developed sense of self-preservation!

136/167	King
150/152	Norfolk

152 'I have evidence that . . .'
The suggestion that More was capable of taking bribes gets short shrift from Norfolk. He may now consider More to be a 'crank' but he finds the suggestion that he was corrupt to be ludicrous.

149/155	Cromwell
151/154	Norfolk

153 'What! Goddammit he . . .'
Norfolk's comments point to the widespread corruption that existed in the administration of law at that time. As such it is a wry comment on More's determination to use the law as protection for himself, and points to the almost inevitable failure of his plan. Note the unequivocal character reference that Norfolk gives More here.

146/155	More
144/155	Law

154 'Indeed yes, we're . . .'
The savage reaction of Norfolk to Rich's remark clearly shows that he was no friend of Rich, nor had he ever been one. It also suggests that he felt angry that such an unworthy person as Rich was attempting to prove More to be corrupt. Note the subtle variations there are in the concepts of friendship and loyalty. Norfolk would not consider Rich a friend, but would he consider More to be one?

145/155	Friendship
152/158	Norfolk
116/157	Rich

155 'And got an impeccably . . .'
Cromwell admits that More's judgment on the woman was 'impeccably correct'. He is only concerned with the gift, for it was More's act of accepting it that might put More within his reach. It is perhaps ironic that, like More, he hopes to use the letter of the law to serve his purpose. Unlike More, he will do what Roper once advocated in the pursuit of justice – can you remember what it was?

152/156	Cromwell
154/156	Friendship
153/164	Law
153/162	More

156 'And got an impeccably . . .'
In what sense does Cromwell use the word 'friend' here?

| 155/158 | Cromwell |
| 155/159 | Friendship |

157 'No, sir!'
The silver goblet, given so long ago to Rich, features for the third time. It also leads to the reintroduction of Matthew, More's Steward, who, along with Rich, and for a price, is also prepared to forget such loyalty as is owed to More.

145/165	Matthew
154/158	Rich
144/161	Structure

158 'Well, make an effort.'
Cromwell has overestimated Rich and underestimated Norfolk – his case against More is defeated by Norfolk's intervention and Rich's poor attention to detail. Note how when Rich looks to Cromwell for guidance 'he gets none'. Cromwell senses that Norfolk is about to demolish Rich's evidence and therefore does not want to be too closely linked to it. He therefore callously and coldly abandons Rich when Norfolk begins his attack on it. Did Rich expect Cromwell to help, and was he prepared then to start lying in order to 'improve' the evidence?

156/160	Cromwell
154/159	Norfolk
157/163	Rich

159 'Look here, Cromwell, . . .'
Why does Norfolk wish to withdraw from this case? Is it his loyalty to More, or can he see that Cromwell will not let the matter drop and is therefore afraid that he will become implicated in it? Is it self-preservation or friendship that prompts his remark, or a combination of the two?

| 156/160 | Friendship |
| 158/161 | Norfolk |

160 'We feel that, . . .'
The smooth way that Cromwell makes his words sound like a threat should warn us that, whilst he underestimates the ease with which he feels More may be persuaded to support the King, he will not give up the attempt. Suddenly, 'friendship' and 'loyalty' have become threatening words as far as Norfolk is concerned, but they will also be used to 'window-dress' the prosecution of More and 'prove' the lack of prejudice in the case against him.

| 158/161 | Cromwell |
| 159/165 | Friendship |

161 'My *dear* Norfolk . . .'
Can you remember the last occasion these very words 'This isn't Spain' were

| 160/162 | Cromwell |

used, by whom and in what circumstances? Are there any similarities between the occasion of their first use and now?

159/194	Norfolk
157/169	Structure

162 'Sir Thomas is . . .'

We normally associate More with imagery relating to the dry land. The image of a 'slippery fish' and nets with 'finer mesh' suggest that More is in deep and dangerous waters and will need to wriggle very energetically indeed if he is to escape from Cromwell's intention to catch him.

161/164	Cromwell
155/169	More
144/189	Imagery

163 'I'm only anxious . . .'

Rich is still rather worried about the whole affair. His unfortunate experience with Norfolk and Cromwell's furious reaction suggest that a failure on his part could be disastrous for him. No doubt he still remembers the incident with Cromwell and the candle.

158/165	Rich

164 'Yes, Richard, I know.'

Cromwell mentions two alternatives available through the law; has he intentionally not mentioned a third? That he will be driven to go outside the law demonstrates the strength of More's case and the weakness of his own, but More's will 'only' be a moral victory.

162/179	Cromwell
155/173	Law

165 'No, sir, but about . . .'

Rich has obviously 'bought' Matthew's services with the promise of a position with him. Note how he uses his new-found power of patronage in an attempt to punish Matthew for his previous insolence. However, he is no match for Matthew who sees him as an easily manipulated fool. How accurate is Matthew's estimation of Rich? Would Matthew ever feel any loyalty was owed to Rich?

160/167	Friendship
163/181	Rich
157/0	Matthew

Scene 3

166 'My husband is coming . . .'

Notice the new and drab setting of More's house. Alice's coarse apron signifies her new poverty and the extent to which More's fortunes have changed. However, the fact that Chapuys visits More indicates that he is still a force to be reckoned with and that powerful people want to have him on their side. Why do you think Alice suggests that Chapuys should go before her husband comes to meet him? Is she afraid that this is a new attempt to persuade More to become involved in affairs of State – an involvement that would be very dangerous?

143/175	Alice

167 ' "Thus it is . . ." '

Can you recall the import of Henry's message to More when the latter resigned his post? Do the circumstances in which More now lives say anything about the message and its contents?

165/173	Friendship
151/172	King

168 'Goodness presents its . . .'
It is ironic that in recognizing More's intrinsic goodness, Chapuys should find this very quality 'difficult'. Does it say much for the course of action which he would like More to take?

149/169	Conscience

169 'Excellency, is he really . . .'
Can you recall when a similar conversation took place between Cromwell and Norfolk? It is ironic that both parties assume that because More has not come out 'against' them, he must be 'for' them. Is the 'third alternative', to which neither Cromwell nor Chapuys admits, in reality the loyalty and duty which More owes to his 'self' and his 'conscience'?

138/172	Chapuys
168/170	Conscience
162/171	More
161/208	Structure
134/197	Self

170 'I wish your mother . . .'
Perhaps the key to Chapuys' and Cromwell's misreading of More is contained in this sentence. Do they both only ever consider the political realities of life on this earth, and ignore the higher religious realities and life after death? What evidence is there in the play as to which of the realities More is concerned with?

169/190	Conscience

171 *Enter* More. *His* . . .
More is now dressed shabbily to indicate his decline in fortune after resigning the Chancellorship.

169/172	More

172 'It is in no . . .'
More still feels that by not actively opposing the King he will escape the hostility of the State. He refuses to open or even touch the letter Chapuys bears from King Charles. Note how Chapuys confirms a comment by Cromwell regarding More's silence, which 'echoes' across Europe.

167/187	King
171/173	More
169/174	Chapuys

173 'You misunderstand me.'
Despite his reduced circumstances, More is still loyal to the Crown. It comes as something of a shock to Chapuys that More is prepared to hand over the letter to the King of England, as loyalty and the law would require. Chapuys is playing a purely political game for political advantage. What sort of 'game' is More playing, and what 'advantage' does he hope to gain from it?

167/181	Friendship
164/180	Law
172/174	More

174 'The man's utterly . . .'
Chapuys' assessment of More's 'lack of reliability' is simply the result of his own failure to understand him. It is not that More has changed his stance, but that the expectations which Chapuys took for certainties, have been rebuffed by More.

172/287	Chapuys
173/175	More

175 'We couldn't come . . .'
The family are reduced to such poverty that they resort to burning bracken to keep warm. There is a deal of sharpness in Alice's comment. It picks up the same theme of her previous criticisms. Despite More's explanation of why he cannot confide some matters to her, she still deeply resents the fact.

166/242	Alice
174/176	More

176 'We couldn't come . . .'
More refuses payment from the Church for his books as he fears the danger of his acceptance of it being misinterpreted – by whom, do you think?

175/177   More

177 'Oh, am I not . . .'
Is More a man who deals in appearance? We would have thought not, but does he imply here that by relying on his silence in the matter of the King's divorce and allowing others to interpret his attitude for themselves (an interpretation based on that silence) he is effectively dealing in appearances? Does this worry him?

176/178   More

178 'I don't think . . .'
Note the irony of this comment, which is followed shortly by an ominous announcement from Roper.

177/179   More

179 'Well, that's all right.'
More's silence has not been enough for Cromwell. More is called to appear before the Secretary to answer charges. How hopeful, and unrealistic, had More been in hoping not to be called to account?

164/180   Cromwell
178/180   More

180 'They say he's . . .'
A few moments before there was considerable emphasis on 'wit', in all senses of the word. It is ironic that More appears not to have the wit to recognize the type of man he is dealing with, believing that his wit and knowledge of the law will be sufficient to save him. In recognizing that Cromwell is a pragmatist, does he not fail to appreciate that if Cromwell cannot achieve his aims legally, he may well adopt less lawful methods? Does he underestimate Cromwell, or fail to understand him, much as Cromwell does with More?

179/181   More
179/182   Cromwell
173/182   Law

Scene 4

181 'Indeed yes, we're . . .'
How would you interpret More's suggestion that he and Rich are old friends? Is he being ironic? Would you agree that there seems to be an implied criticism of Rich in his assertion? Note that Rich has now obtained the costume he wanted to signify rank and office. One wonders what he has 'sold' to purchase the office from Cromwell.

180/182   More
165/191   Rich
173/194   Friendship

182 'Make a note of . . .'
Cromwell's motives in this jocular approach to More are quite obvious. He is trying to put More off his guard. You may be sure that, despite his instruction to Rich that there was no need to record the conversation yet, it would be recorded if More made any statement which Cromwell could use against him. On the other hand, More is being very cold and cautious. His legal mind will follow every word uttered and respond with great caution, as indicated here.

180/183   Cromwell
181/184   More
180/186   Law

		Characters and ideas previous/next comment

183 'Sir Thomas, Sir . . .'
The events about to unfold will suggest that Cromwell's comment about More having been '*in*' the world and now '*so much*' retired from it, is perhaps more perceptive and prophetically ironic than he realizes.

182/184   Cromwell

184 'Yet do you know . . .'
Cromwell is here emphasizing the loneliness of More's position. Looking at the people and institutions who have supported the King's action we can begin to appreciate the great determination and strength of conviction that More must have.

183/185   Cromwell
182/185   More

185 'You admit meeting her.'
Note this comment of Cromwell's about More meeting the 'Holy Maid of Kent': it is almost a charge. Norfolk will shortly admit that it is becoming dangerous to talk to More. More's role as judge has been reversed to that of accused and his future is as fraught with danger as was the 'Holy Maid's'. Perhaps her eventual fate is meant to warn us of what will happen to More.

184/186   More
184/186   Cromwell

186 'You have been . . .'
More has given the first indication to Cromwell of the care and scrupulous honesty with which he conducted his professional affairs. This really ought to have been obvious to Cromwell from the affair of the silver goblet.

185/187   Cromwell
185/187   More
182/188   Law

187 'Do you deny that . . .'
Cromwell's second charge against More is easily refuted (that is, disproved). Note how More demonstrates his knowledge of the King and thus the resultant worthlessness of the accusation. Is it possible that this moment would stay in Cromwell's mind? If the King would not perjure himself, perhaps someone else could be persuaded to commit perjury with an equally desirable effect?

186/188   Cromwell
186/188   More
172/188   King

188 'Then know that . . .'
The charge which Cromwell now levels against More, if indeed it comes from the King, is the most dangerous even if it is not indictable under law. If the King accused him of being a 'traitorous subject', then his fate really is sealed.

187/191   King
187/189   Cromwell
187/189   More
186/202   Law

189 'Oh yes.'
Cromwell would appear to think less of More now. In his view More's silence has 'echoed' across Europe thereby giving a lead to all those who object to the King's actions – that is the 'gale' More has raised. However, unlike those who take the lead they think More has given them, he keeps silent and refuses to stand up for his beliefs – staying safe in 'harbour'. Note the imagery used: the dangers of the open sea and the safety of harbour. Is this a fair assessment of the case and a fair judgment on More? You might like to consider whether it is More's fault if people choose to put interpretations on his silence and then act on those interpretations as though he had encouraged them. For an example of this bear in mind how Cromwell and Chapuys viewed More's actions: 'if he opposes Spain, he supports us', 'if he's opposed to Cromwell, he's for us'. How can we hold More responsible for both views?

188/190   More
188/190   Cromwell
162/193   Imagery

190 'No, he's misusing . . .'
Cromwell equates intelligence with pragmatism. He feels More ought to realize he cannot win against the King and should therefore bow to the King's wishes. Intelligence has very little to do with More's decision – the key lies with conscience.

170/191	Conscience
189/191	Cromwell
189/193	More

191 'Oh, be quiet, Rich . . .'
Note how Cromwell presents the King's idea of conscience – or maybe it is Cromwell's interpretation! It's a rather brutal 'bless my marriage' or be destroyed; you serve me or you are against me. It rather suggests the image alluded to at the start of the play, of Adam being unable to serve both God and the Devil, and it also reflects the conflict that is in More's mind. He believes he has a higher duty to his God than to the King, and his conscience tells him that in this case he must serve what he sees as God's wishes, not the King's. Whichever way it is viewed, the choice is stark.

188/198	King
181/225	Rich
190/192	Conscience
190/192	Cromwell

192 'Oh, there's no . . .'
In Cromwell's last speech he indulged in a particularly good example of 'double-talk'. Simply put, it means 'if the King does it, it must be right'. It is Cromwell's job to ensure that More pays for his lack of 'loyalty' to the King, and that the punishment leaves the King with a clear conscience. Cromwell's final statement about being keepers of the King's conscience, and 'it's ravenous' do not bode well for More.

191/194	Conscience
191/203	Cromwell

Scene 5

193 'Boat! . . . Boat! . . .'
The fact that no one will carry More on the river, which has been frequently used as a symbol of danger, further emphasizes his isolation. Following the lead of their 'betters', the Common Man is also disassociating himself from More – now a dangerous man to know.

43/0	Boatman
189/200	Imagery
190/194	More

194 'Probably. . . . So listen . . .'
Even the powerful Duke of Norfolk does not feel safe in these dangerous times. He recognizes the lack of force that his comment about 'not behaving like a gentleman' has, but still feels the appeal to friendship may have more. However, what does he mean by the obligations of friendship in this context? It would seems that knowing More puts his friend at risk. Should that be a reason for More to go against his conscience?

192/196	Conscience
193/195	More
161/195	Norfolk
181/195	Friendship

195 'I can't relieve you . . .'
One of the keys to More's lack of openness to his family is his concern for their welfare. Should he be convicted of treason then all his family possessions would be lost. By not confiding his thoughts to them, they cannot be used against him. His comment to Norfolk, 'you have a son' is much to the point.

194/196	Friendship
194/196	More
194/196	Norfolk

196 'Oh, that's immutable is it?'
Norfolk's comment here highlights much of the mistaken thinking about More's actions and attitudes. They do not understand that it is not a matter

195/197	More
195/198	Norfolk

of More perversely 'refusing' to give in, he is 'unable' to give in, his conscience will not allow him. Unlike Cromwell, who a little earlier suggests that it is he and Rich who must effectively rule the King's conscience, More's conscience rules More's actions – a crucial distinction.

195/199	Friendship
194/202	Conscience

197 'To me it *has* . . .'

A man cannot serve two masters is what More is saying here. His affection for Norfolk is deep, but his love for God is absolute and brooks no interference, no matter what earthly reason may be advanced. More's love for God *is* More; it is the whole reason for everything he does, and every moment he lives. For More, God is love, and God is life. Given the earthbound considerations of power and money that rule the rest of men, it is not really surprising that they totally fail to understand him.

196/198	More
169/201	Self

198 'And who are you?'

Norfolk concedes that the aristocracy of England have given in to the King's will. The 'arrogant . . . proud, splenetic ones' have accepted the King's 'rule', so why can't More? The answer is simply that More puts God's 'rule' above that of the King, and More has accepted God's 'rule'. Norfolk's anguished comment 'You'll break my heart' foreshadows the emotional appeals that will be made to More by his family. They tear at More's emotions, but cannot compete with the greater loyalty he has to God's love. Whether or not you agree with the reasons suggested for More's actions, and whether or not you believe in God, you have to understand that for More, God is real, his obligations to God are real and having formed that 'certain conscience', he has to follow it.

191/226	King
197/199	More
196/199	Norfolk

199 'Oh, that can be . . .'

More's declaration that Norfolk's friendship for him can be broken is important. The theme of friendship has been one about which all the players in this drama have had something to say. Now, More is to put its strength to the test.

198/200	More
198/209	Norfolk
196/201	Friendship

200 'The nobility of England, . . .'

The Sermon on the Mount is to be found in the New Testament of the Bible, in the Gospel of Saint Matthew, chapters five to seven. It expresses the noblest of Christian ideals, but you will only catch the full flavour and import of More's picture of the nobility snoring through it if you actually look it up and spare the few minutes needed to read it. Thomas Aquinas was a 13th-century theologian, still famed for his writings on God, the Church, and Christian doctrine. The rich contrast here in the image of nobles snoring their way through the Sermon on the Mount but expending huge amounts of energy on the pedigree of a terrier used to catch rats, is highly insulting.

199/201	More
193/206	Imagery

201 'And what would you . . .'

Read this passage carefully. It is one of those occasions on which More attempts to explain what drives him, and how he regards his 'self'. Note the distinction he draws between his 'pride', his 'spleen', his 'appetites' and his 'self'. He is asking a question which is extremely difficult to answer, basically, 'what is the nature of a man?', and he is suggesting that it is something far more real and permanent than mere emotions, appetites – and earthly loyalties.

199/209	Friendship
200/202	More
197/234	Self

202 'Because as you stand, . . .'
More emphasizes that there is a higher court of law than that of the King of England, and one before which all men will have to appear.

196/204	Conscience
188/203	Law
201/205	More

203 'Father, by this Act, . . .'
Cromwell has fulfilled his threat to make laws to support the King's case. Refusal to take the oath will be regarded as treason, and treason, of course, is punishable by death.

199/211	Cromwell
202/204	Law

204 'What is the oath?'
More's concern to know the actual words of the oath, and Roper's contemptuous 'we know what it will mean', reflect the argument that has raged to date about the meaning of More's silence. More is very aware that if the oath has been carelessly worded he might just be able to take it and escape from a very difficult situation without offending his conscience.

202/217	Conscience
203/210	Law

205 'I spoke, slightingly, . . .'
More suggests that wit, in the sense of intellectual ability, is given by God to man as a means to escape from earthly dilemmas. But of course, that 'means' does not necessarily guarantee the 'escape' will be successful!

202/207	More

Scene 6

206 '*Now* look! . . . I don't . . .'
The instruments of interrogation and torture have been lowered onto the stage which remains symbolically lit as water, emphasizing the peril that More is in. The Common Man makes a passing but cynical reference to the idea that those who seek after truth through the use of torture, find the process as painful as those they torture. One can but doubt the assertion!

200/230	Imagery
0/207	Jailer

207 'They'd let him out . . .'
In referring to 'the old adage' the Jailer points to the fact that he, in common with many, finds it difficult to see beyond the realities of life on this earth. Note the stark contrast with More's resolute stand in the face of opposition.

206/208	Jailer
205/212	More

208 *An envelope descends . . .*
Note the peculiar way in which the letter appears, the contents of which acquaint us with the eventual fate of all those present, with one important exception – More. Would you consider that they all get their just deserts? To what extent would you say that More's view of there being a final justice at God's hands, gives a better chance of everyone getting their 'just deserts'? Note the device of a bell to pull the action back into 'real' time.

207/222	Jailer
169/223	Structure

209 'A chair for the . . .'
How would you assess Norfolk's action in calling for a chair for More? Does friendship or pity influence his action?

201/211	Friendship
199/210	Norfolk

210 'A chair for the . . .'
Cromwell's earlier contention that Norfolk's involvement in More's trial

204/212	Law

	Characters and ideas	
	previous/next comment	

would give it an air of respectability has been put into practice. Norfolk heads the Seventh Commission to enquire into Thomas More: unexpected and prolonged interrogation is still recognized as a form of torture.

209/211	Norfolk

211 'Thomas, we must . . .'
Note how the remains of Norfolk's old friendship with More softens his approach. Why do you think this makes Cromwell so angry?

203/219	Cromwell
219/216	Norfolk
209/216	Friendship

212 'Sir Thomas, it states . . .'
Here, for the first time, we see in action that principle of silence which More advocates.

210/213	Law
207/213	More

213 'The law requires . . .'
More is a lawyer and it will soon become apparent that, on points of law, he has no match in this court.

212/214	More
212/215	Law

214 'I cannot judge . . .'
The one thing that More has clung to is the fact that his conscience tells him he cannot support the King's action. In that respect, above all others, he has a very clear conscience. When Cranmer attacks his 'spiritual standing' with absolutely no evidence to support his criticism, More is justifiably furious.

213/215	More
0/218	Cranmer

215 'It's most material.'
Read this speech carefully. More gives a very clear explanation of the legal position.

214/216	More
213/219	Law

216 'Oh, confound all this . . .'
Norfolk finds the idea of executing More repulsive. He has a very limited grasp of More's motives and, despite the previous explanations given by More, he urges him to take the oath merely out of friendship, an appeal that More finds very moving but still unacceptable.

215/217	More
211/224	Norfolk
211/260	Friendship

217 'And when we stand . . .'
For More, the ultimate choice is paradise or eternal damnation. If he does not follow his conscience then damnation will be his reward. Quite reasonably, he prefers paradise.

204/218	Conscience
216/219	More

218 'So those of us . . .'
Cranmer's intervention here enables More to make the point that all men have a conscience; how they respond to its dictates is not something he can judge. He can only respond to his own conscience.

217/222	Conscience
214/223	Cranmer

219 'Oh, justice is what . . .'
It seems clear that More and Cromwell have two differing notions of justice. More is referring to the fair application of the legal statutes of the law of the land, without fear or favour. Cromwell's response suggests that he sees justice as the execution of More, for the King's convenience, and, if necessary, despite the law.

211/220	Cromwell
215/250	Law
217/220	More

220 'Might I have one . . .'
Cromwell objects to More having access to books. He has been in the Tower of London for a year: how important would books have been in preserving More's sanity? Note that Cromwell's reaction is not just pettiness. He recognizes the intellectual and spiritual comfort a man such as More would have gained from them and how they would help prolong his determination to resist Cromwell.

219/221	Cromwell
219/221	More

221 'May I see . . .'
Note Cromwell's blank refusal to allow More to see his family. It is a cruel decision, but is it cruelty just for the sake of it? In answering this question, bear in mind the comment just made about access to books.

220/224	Cromwell
220/224	More

222 'Place your left hand . . .'
Can you see the irony in the administration of this oath following the recent conversation? More was making the exact point that it was his immortal soul's fate which was his prime concern. Here the fate of the jailer's immortal soul is used as a 'guarantee' of his honesty in spying on More. Note how the State uses the Church's authority in the administration of an oath; but what meaning does it have for More's prosecutors?

218/226	Conscience
208/223	Jailer

223 'And there's fifty . . .'
Fifty guineas would have been an enormous amount of money in those times. Are we to believe Cranmer's hasty denial that it is to tempt the Jailer into perjury? Perhaps he did not have perjury in mind, but what about Cromwell? Note how this offer picks up on a previous conversation Cromwell had with Rich. The Jailer obviously feels the fifty guineas is offered as a bribe and sensibly decides to remain 'deaf'. Is this out of consideration for More, or self-protection? When did the Common Man have a similar experience of becoming 'deaf'? Note also how this event echoes all those other times when the Common Man is on the receiving end of 'additional payments'.

218/284	Cranmer
222/239	Jailer
208/231	Structure

224 'Tomorrow morning, remove . . .'
Cromwell orders the removal of all More's books. Reread comment 220 to see why he does this. Consider also why Norfolk opposes the act. Note how Cromwell's survival is inextricably bound up with the 'success' of this trial.

221/225	Cromwell
221/226	More
216/260	Norfolk

225 'The Attorney General for . . .'
Rich is still ambitious and asks Cromwell to secure his appointment as Attorney General for Wales. His appetite for power is obviously growing; however, bearing in mind the seniority of the post he will have to 'pay' a considerable amount for the promotion. You might remember this when Rich enters as a key witness against More in the trial proper.

224/226	Cromwell
191/269	Rich

226 'Oh, not *now* . . .'
Cromwell considers the use of torture on More, but as quickly rejects it. Why do you think the King would not permit it? Is he perhaps suffering from an 'attack of conscience'?

222/259	Conscience
225/227	Cromwell
198/247	King
224/228	More

Scene 7

227 'Wake up Sir Thomas!'
Why has More's family been allowed to visit him? Do Cromwell's last words, 'We have to find some gentler way' have a bearing on the matter, and if so, how?

228 'Margaret! What's this?'
More's first reaction is that of fear. One of the things he has attempted to do from the start is to keep his family ignorant of his opinions and therefore safe from persecution.

229 Roper *is staring* . . .
This is the first time that Roper comes face to face with the realities of following one's conscience, as More has done. The presence of the rack, an instrument of torture which was used to 'stretch' a prisoner, makes him realize just what might be involved for More.

230 'It drips!'
The reintroduction of the river as an image, with the accompanying description 'It drips!', serves to reiterate the danger which has always been associated with water throughout the play.

231 'And a bottle of wine.'
Can you remember the last time More was served wine, and by whom? The circumstances are rather different now, and his jocular 'Is it good . . .' is in no way meant to suggest that Roper was like Matthew. It does, however, provide a nice structural link with the earlier scene.

232 'Sir, come out! Swear . . .'
Roper blurts out the reason for their visit and reveals that Margaret has taken an oath in an attempt to persuade More to swear to the Act of Succession. You will recall Cromwell's quest for a 'gentler way'; presumably, this is it.

233 'Then say the words . . .'
This is the first of Margaret's attempts to persuade her father to change his mind. Note what her argument is based on.

234 'Then it's a poor . . .'
In response to Margaret's argument More considers that a man's soul, his self, is a gift of God and is always in need of care. It is as vulnerable as water cupped in one's hands, and once lost it is gone for ever. One may fool others by saying a false oath, but not God, to whom the oath is addressed. Hence, More has to reject Margaret's suggestion.

235 'In any state that . . .'
Margaret's next argument has echoes of a previous scene. Do you remember the conversation between Rich and More about 'suffering'? Look back to see how close this present conversation is to it.

	Characters and ideas previous/next comment	
	226/239	Cromwell
	226/230	More
	140/231	Roper
	206/234	Imagery
	228/231	More
	230/232	More
	229/272	Roper
	223/247	Structure
	231/234	More
	140/234	Margaret
	233/235	Margaret
	232/236	More
	201/265	Self
	230/241	Imagery
	234/237	Margaret

	Characters and ideas previous/next comment	

236 'That's very neat.'
More's answer has a fuller echo of the response he gave to Norfolk earlier in the play after his first meeting with Rich and Cromwell. Can you see how?

234/237   More

237 'Content? If they'd open . . .'
Do you recall the remark at the start of the play about Adam? This reference to 'Eve [running] out of apples' refers to the arguments Margaret is putting before More in an effort to tempt him away from his principles. However, unlike Adam, More is determined not to 'fall'.

235/238   Margaret
236/238   More

238 'The King's more . . .'
Why is news of his family's abject poverty more hurtful to More than even the rack could be? It was obviously Cromwell's intention to use the family to break More's will. He reckoned without the strength of More's conviction.

237/240   Margaret
237/282   More

239 'Two minutes to go . . .'
The very limited time More has been granted with his family is an act of cruelty. Why do you think Cromwell decided to make it so short?

227/250   Cromwell
223/240   Jailer

240 'Anyhow!–Have you . . .'
More attempts to 'buy' extra time with his family. Note, though, that he tells Roper not to try to bribe the Jailer, and to share the wine. Even in this desperate situation of trying to gain more time with his family he insists on correctness.

239/247   Jailer
238/241   More

241 'It makes no difference, . . .'
More instructs his family to flee the country. The sea is a barrier to their safety. To lessen the chances of discovery More instructs them to go from different ports. He is obviously of the opinion that he will be executed for treason, despite the law, and that his family will also be persecuted – not an unusual event in those days.

234/247   Imagery
240/243   More

242 'By God, you think . . .'
Alice has had little to say so far in this meeting. Obviously, the family were hoping that Margaret's words would bring the desired result. With knowledge of her failure, Alice is faced with defeat and strikes out at her husband, not in hate, but in bitterness at the prospect of losing him.

175/244   Alice

243 'Alice, if you can . . .'
Cromwell's plan to change More's mind has not worked, but he has certainly caused him a great deal of heartache and anguish. The relationship between More and his wife has always been rather overshadowed by his regard for his clever Margaret. Here, the full force of his love for Alice is seen.

241/245   More

244 'S-s-sh. . . . As for . . .'
Alice may not understand the intellectual reasoning behind More's stance but she does 'understand' the man. She recognizes his innate goodness and is prepared to take the rest on faith. She is unhappy that God has 'kept deadly quiet' but retains her faith in Him. For the King and his court she has unbounded contempt.

242/0   Alice

245 'Why, it's a lion . . .'
The King referred to himself as a lion. Do you think that Alice is much more
worthy of the title? Happy in the knowledge that Alice does not hate him,
More has time even at this moment to think of Bishop Fisher, who is also
imprisoned.

243/246   More

246 'Now do as I . . .'
More's generosity to his friend and fellow sufferer Bishop Fisher increases
the sympathy the audience feel for his own suffering.

245/248   More

247 'Don't put your . . .'
Do you remember the previous reference to mud by Henry? Now the
Common Man is also described as muddy. Is it reasonable to see these two
images as linking the highest and lowest in the land. Do both stand equally
'besmirched'?

241/250   Imagery
240/248   Jailer
226/274   King
231/252   Structure

248 'You understand my position, . . .'
More's passionate outburst against 'plain, simple men' expresses his
contempt for them. He feels they have abandoned all principles to
compromise and self-preservation. Is he also more honest than Cromwell,
Rich, Norfolk and the rest who have supported the King? The Jailer 'just
wants to keep out of trouble', the others seem to hide behind law,
friendship or loyalty, but basically they are also just keeping out of trouble
without any reference to the rights or wrongs of what they are doing or
whom they harm.

247/0   Jailer
246/256   More

Scene 8

249 *Immediately: (1) Music,* . . .
The scene is changed to a Court of Law. The Common Man changes his
clothes and becomes yet another character.

119/288   Common Man

250 'What Englishman can . . .'
Note how Cromwell's piece of rhetoric combines the image of water, nearly
always associated in the play with danger, with law. The line 'The Canvas
and the Rigging of the Law' is quite revealing; canvasses can be painted in
many colours and we only have to consider the colloquial meaning of 'to rig
something' to realize the way in which Cromwell's words mean quite the
opposite of what they seem to say.

239/251   Cromwell
247/251   Imagery
219/251   Law

251 'Forbidden here the galley-master's . . .'
More did not suffer any direct physical abuse, the 'galley-master's whip'
was 'forbidden', but he had just spent a considerable amount of time in
prison, suffering mental torture because, metaphorically, he had the
'strength of oak' to follow the dictates of his conscience. Would you consider
that Cromwell, Rich or Norfolk have acted as though they had 'Hearts of
Oak'?

250/254   Cromwell
250/254   Imagery
250/254   Law

252 *Above the two rows . . .*
The stage instructions show the jury as a collection of hats hanging from a pair of wires. Amongst the hats are those of the Steward, Boatman, Innkeeper and Jailer. Does the jury's lack of real people suggest that perhaps they won't be 'judging' a real trial?

0/253	Foreman
247/254	Structure

253 *'Foreman of the . . .'*
All the jury have the same grey hats. Like the people whom the hats represent, they are drab and colourless. There is no distinction between one hat and another, they are faceless puppets and 'the cap fits'.

252/0	Foreman

254 *'So, now we'll . . .'*
Cromwell's cynical and rhetorical speech in rhyming couplets makes a mockery of the process of law. The 'good plain sailor' echoes the Jailer's 'plain simple man', and we know what More thought of him! Again we have the reference to 'fixing' something, and it is totally ironic that Cromwell should suggest that a quicksand can be fixed. What he is really suggesting is that the process of law that is about to be paraded in front of us is an absolute sham.

251/257	Cromwell
251/255	Law
252/272	Structure
251/263	Imagery

255 *'Sir Thomas More, you . . .'*
The trial begins and More's worst fears are realized: he is charged with treason. Even at this moment, the chance of escaping his fate is held out to him if he will only take the oath.

254/256	Law

256 *'My lords, I thank you.'*
More's prolonged suffering and imprisonment have led him to fear he may not have the strength to use his wit to protect himself. Such 'show trials' where the accused is not fit enough to present a reasonable defence are not unknown in some countries during our own times.

255/262	Law
248/258	More

257 *'It is the same . . .'*
Cromwell's callous announcement of Bishop Fisher's execution for the same charge causes More considerable distress. Is Cromwell just being cruel, or still desperately hoping to persuade More to change his mind?

254/261	Cromwell

258 *'Silence is not denial.'*
More again protests that silence is not denial. Despite his previous hope that his safety lay in silence, he is beginning to realize that law and justice are not available in this court, as the trial has been rigged.

256/260	More

259 *'Death . . . comes for us . . .'*
Does More sense that the King might be present somewhere, and listening? Certainly, such plain but self-evident truths are not the ones normally flung in the face of a king, and certainly not in the words that More uses. Perhaps he hopes to show his judges that the fate awaiting kings will also await them. The central point of his speech is that real judgment, God's judgment, comes after earthly death, and all will be subject to it.

226/264	Conscience

260 *'Your life lies . . .'*
Norfolk is still trying to save his old friend, but More, perhaps realizing more

258/262	More

224/277	Norfolk
216/277	Friendship

than ever that his fate is sealed, cannot take the easy way out and hope for the natural death of old age.

---

261 'But, Gentlemen of the . . .'

This long speech by Cromwell considers three 'cases' of silence. The silence of death, he says, is absolute. The silence that does not warn of, or protest against, an evil act supports that act. Would you consider here that More's belief is that the King's act is evil, and that, on Cromwell's reasoning, More ought therefore to be considered as agreeing with the King? Cromwell's first point about the silence of death is perhaps self-evident; his second would suggest that More is innocent. What does his third point suggest?

257/266	Cromwell

---

262 'Not so, Mr Secretary . . .'

Despite More's weakness and long period of suffering his affirmation of points of law is eloquent and clever. Cromwell's response to the point of law that More advances is a fairly feeble cry that More makes the law 'murky', when in fact he is explaining it with great clarity and force.

256/263	Law
260/266	More

---

263 'The law is not . . .'

Note the image More uses here of the law being a causeway which enables a traveller to pass between perilous waters. It contrasts strongly with the corrupt images of law which Cromwell used at the beginning of the trial.

262/271	Law
254/0	Imagery

---

264 'The conscience, the . . .'

Cromwell's reaction to More's introduction of the word 'conscience' is one of scorn, which brings about an equally scornful reply from More. The use of the word has been twisted in some circumstances to become a form of abuse; think about the term 'conscientious objector'. In the last two world wars such people have been the subject of abuse from their fellows because they would not kill for their country; they were looked upon as traitors and cowards. Look ahead some lines to see how Cromwell uses a variation of this abuse when he trots out the same jingoistic rhetoric (that is, speech which is showy and exaggerated) of '. . . State! . . . King! In a great native country!'.

259/266	Conscience

---

265 'It is not so, . . .'

More sees his action as an attempt to save his soul. Cromwell has a very much more limited view of 'self'; for him it represents only the physical body of man.

234/0	Self

---

266 'A miserable thing, . . .'

Cromwell's view is that a man's soul is not as important as loyalty to the King, State and country. Do you think Cromwell's motives are simply ones of loyalty?

264/267	Conscience
261/271	Cromwell
262/270	More

---

267 'Can I help my . . .'

More is unable to ignore the dictates of his conscience. He cannot lie for the sake of King or country. It is ironic that immediately after his dignified rebuttal of how useless his lies would be to his King, Rich is called to give evidence. How useful to the King will Rich's lies be?

266/0	Conscience

268 'My lords, I wish . . .'
Rich appears dressed as Attorney General for Wales – a title he has accepted in return for giving false evidence against More. Do you recall his words to More at the beginning of the play 'I want a gown like yours'? He now has it, but would More consider he paid the right price for it?

225/269   Rich

269 'I do solemnly swear . . .'
Note the ironic little touch of Rich 'forgetting' to ask for God's help.

268/270   Rich

270 'He said "Parliament has . . ." '
Rich's perjury brings only pity from More. It is ironic that when More *does* take an oath, something which is so very important to him and, in his view, to God, it should be ruled as being unacceptable by the State and inadmissible as a defence in a court of law.

266/272   More
269/273   Rich

271 'There were two . . .'
Note how carefully Cromwell has rigged his evidence. Two important witnesses to the conversation between More and Rich have been 'sent' to Ireland. Without the possibility of examining them More is deprived of the opportunity to break their stories and thus prove Rich a liar. It does not take much imagination to guess who sent them to Ireland.

266/272   Cromwell
263/272   Law

272 'To what purpose?'
More fears the precedent set by his case. Think back to his argument with Roper about the thickets of law, and Roper's view that he would cut them down in the pursuit of 'justice'. This has just happened, but has justice been served?

271/274   Cromwell
271/275   Law
270/274   More
231/0   Roper
254/278   Structure

273 'For Wales?'
More's comment on Rich's action is accurate, as was his assessment of Rich's character at the start of the play.

270/0   Rich

274 'Now I must ask . . .'
Note that the King still gives More the chance to save his life by taking the Oath of Succession even after being found guilty of high treason – do you imagine Henry feels he has much on his conscience with regard to More?

272/287   Cromwell
247/275   King
272/275   More

275 'Yes. . . . To avoid this . . .'
Having been found guilty and knowing that his life has been forfeited, More at last feels able to break his silence. In a few, direct words, he outlines the grounds on which he feels he must reject the actions of King and Parliament: the man-made laws are in direct opposition to the laws of God, and the 'earthly' King is attempting to take 'spiritual power' – in the sense of taking control over the spiritual life of his people. More further reminds the Court that the actions of the King also violate his own Coronation oath and the provisions of the Magna Carta. The Magna Carta is a document, established in 1215 by King John, which is generally held to be the basis for the rights and freedoms of the English people. The first part of that document outlines the rights of the Church, rights which the King has now overturned.

272/278   Law
274/276   More
274/0   King

Characters and ideas: a two-column reference list appears on the right margin, with previous/next comment numbers.

276 'Not so, Mr Secretary!'
Rejecting Cromwell's assertion that he is malicious, More continues his explanation for his actions. After restating his loyalty to the King and affirming that he has neither done nor thought harm to anyone, he turns to the crux of the reason for his appearance in court: Henry wanted his support for his marriage to Anne Boleyn, and, unable to persuade More to give him that support, he has effectively connived in this rigged prosecution.

275/277 More

277 'Prisoner at the bar, . . .'
It is ironic that More's old friend is appointed to pronounce sentence of death on him. It does, however, indicate the degree of importance that Norfolk places on his own head as opposed to the friendship he had for More. There is no doubt that he would decline an invitation to join More, 'for fellowship'.

276/281 More
260/280 Friendship
260/280 Norfolk

278 *The scene change* . . .
Note how the stage directions refer to the 'trappings' of justice. The word indicates that whilst there had been all the appearances of a properly conducted trial, in reality it has been a farce. There was no justice, just the 'trappings'. It may be seen as rather ironic that More, who placed such reliance on the law, should find himself convicted. However, do remember that justice and the law are only as good and reliable as those who administer them. We know how More discharged his obligations in that regard from the words of Norfolk and Cromwell; you can judge for yourself how his opponents discharged their obligations.

275/283 Law
272/279 Structure

Scene 9

279 *When these movements* . . .
The Common Man becomes the Headsman with help from Cromwell who gives him a mask. Think back to all those occasions when the Common Man has featured in the play. Were there any of his various guises that did not have contact with Cromwell? To what extent is there a suggestion here that Cromwell has been symbolic of an evil force that affects all men? As an example of this, consider the avaricious nature of the Common Man, and also of Rich. What was Cromwell's part in feeding their greed?

0/287 Headsman
278/0 Structure

280 'I can come no . . .'
Note Norfolk's words. Again, they ironically reflect Norfolk's plea to More to join him and his fellow lords and Parliamentarians in their support of the King, only this time Norfolk reaffirms his decision not to 'come' with More – to where?

277/281 Friendship
277/281 Norfolk

281 'My master had easel . . .'
More refuses Norfolk's gesture of a final drink of wine. In reminding Norfolk of Christ's final drink of gall, does he identify himself as a Christian martyr? Do bear in mind the parallels which could be drawn with some biblical incidents, particularly that of the robust and staunch friend of Christ, Peter, who denied his Master when Christ was arrested and put on trial. Are there any other parallels you can think of – perhaps with Judas, who betrayed his Master for money?

277/282 More
280/0 Friendship
280/0 Norfolk

282 'Have patience, Margaret, . . .'
More's farewell to Margaret is simple and unsentimental. In this way it has

281/283 More

		Characters and ideas *previous/next comment*

maximum dramatic import. Note how More views death: it is not a thing to fear and he has long since come to terms with its inevitability. What does he mean when he says to Margaret 'You have long known the secrets of my heart'? Is this the death he has always wished for, despite saying that he was not the stuff of which martyrs are made, or is it that he refers to the fact that he has always longed for the moment when he will meet his Maker – the fact of martyrdom being incidental?

238/0   Margaret

283 'Sir Thomas!' . . .
Having said his farewell to his 'friend' Norfolk, and his family, represented by Margaret, he now has his final dealings with those affairs of justice which occupied so many of his days. The sudden appearance of the woman is unexpected. It is not needed, but should there be any uncertainty about his honesty in judging her case, his repetition of his verdict just before his execution should surely lay to rest any doubts.

278/0   Law
282/284   More

284 *Offended*, Cranmer *does* . . .
Cranmer did not loom large in the play, but here, his appearance allows More symbolically to reject the falseness with which he feels this man and his beliefs are tainted. However, do note that there is no bitterness in his refusal and he addresses Cranmer in a manner which is 'quite kindly'. What was Cranmer's eventual fate?

223/285   Cranmer
283/286   More

285 'You're very sure . . .'
Cranmer's remark here points to one of the keys to More's decision not to take the Oath: More is not just sure, he is absolutely certain that what he does is right and that as a result he will now go to his God. Note how Cranmer envies his certainty and calm. One can but wonder at Cranmer's thoughts when he met his death.

284/0   Cranmer

286 'He will not refuse . . .'
Once again More confirms that this is not a moment he now dreads, rather it is one that he is gladly accepting, indeed, welcoming. The huge gulf between the ideals that drove More, and those which provided the spurs for Norfolk, Cromwell, Rich and all the other characters is evidenced here. More's ideal is totally bound up with the spiritual; where do the ideals of his prosecutors find their origin?

284/0   More

287 'Behold – the head – . . .'
It would seem obvious that the Headsman should be referring to More when he talks of a 'traitor'. However, it is ironic that with his words ringing in our ears we should see Chapuys and Cromwell leaving the stage arm in arm, laughing and chuckling together. Chapuys has always seemed to be a supporter of More and has approved of his stand – when he thought More was supporting his cause. This unexpected gesture of friendship between him and Cromwell is sinister and cynical. Is the act of sacrificing principles to political pressure to be admired? Who would you say are the traitors, and to whom?

174/0   Chapuys
274/0   Cromwell
279/0   Headsman

288 'I'm breathing . . .'
The alternative ending is rich in irony. Each member of the audience is reminded of the price they may be paying for keeping alive compromise, sinfulness and denial of one's self or soul. In More's view, it would not be a price worth paying.

249/0   Common Man

Characters in the play

This is a very brief overview of each character. You should use it as a starting point for your own studies of characterization. For each of the aspects of character mentioned you should look in your text for evidence to support or contradict the views expressed here, and indeed, your own views as well.

Know the incidents and conversations which will support and enlarge upon your knowledge of each character. You will find it helpful to select a character and follow the commentary, referring always to the text to read and digest the context of the comment.

Alice

Alice was More's second wife – his first wife Jane, who was the mother of Margaret, died in 1511.

Bolt characterizes her as blunt and direct, not an intellectual but strong in rugged individualism. She is a sort of 'mother-earth' figure whose qualities contrast well with More's lofty intellect and spiritualism and with his educated daughter, Margaret. She does not pretend to understand More or his actions, but her faith in him is such that at the end she is prepared to trust his judgment and accept that he must go his own way.

Chapuys

Chapuys is a Spanish diplomat and staunch Catholic. His duties lie in securing and holding onto Spanish interests, and particularly upholding the validity of Henry's marriage to the Spanish princess, Catherine. He pretends to admire and flatter More but we are aware that his motives are for the furtherance of political convenience rather than friendship.

The conclusion of the play which shows an alliance between the Catholic Chapuys and the English statesman Cromwell, suggests that for these statesmen at least, there is always room for compromise. An aristocrat, he is no less cunning and untrustworthy than Cromwell, who rose from the 'lower classes'.

Common Man: Steward, Boatman, Publican, Jailer, Foreman, Headsman

The Common Man provides narrative linkage between the scenes of the play. He is able to set scenes, describe passages of time, and even forecast events, something which is thought by Bolt to be dramatically appropriate. In directly addressing the audience he also provides a link between them and the play's concerns.

He provides comic relief and occasionally shows some measure of self-awareness throughout the play. If More's great strength is his belief that his 'self' is unchangeable, the Common Man's weakness is in his readiness to adapt and change into almost anything as a means to survive in a turbulent and imperfect world. The succession of characters he portrays provides an image of that fluidity.

In the alternative ending of the play the audience is invited to recognize the quality of the Common Man in themselves and, it follows, to reflect on their own spiritual condition.

Cranmer

Cranmer's character is very lightly drawn. However, the two occasions when he appears enable Bolt to touch briefly upon quite important matters. Read the two scenes carefully.

Cromwell

Cromwell, as depicted by Bolt, is one of a group of men who lived during the Renaissance period (that is, between the 14th and 16th centuries) and who seem to have embraced the ideas of Machiavelli's advice to rulers. In consequence they have become totally unscrupulous in their pursuit of power. We recognize Cromwell's fierce loyalty to the King as being bound up in lesser motives of personal promotion and self-preservation.

Bolt allows him little or no sympathy in the play, and an analysis of Cromwell's comments about More suggests that he is not very perceptive in his reading of such a man's character. What he does successfully, is recognize the weaknesses in men such as Rich and Norfolk. His influence over Rich is blatantly apparent, but you have to look a little more carefully for those few instances where he demonstrates Norfolk's weaknesses. Cromwell shows little professional respect for More's intellect and knowledge of the law, and even less for More's conscience. In the final analysis he demonstrates no great legal, intellectual or other abilities, but he does 'fix' things rather well!

In common with other characters, and in contrast to More, he is afraid of the earthly power wielded by the King.

The King

No man may have absolute power and not be corrupted by it. Bolt's portrayal of the young Henry reveals his dual personality. He is witty, charming and debonair, but dangerous, self-opinionated and cruel. One would have thought that the life imprisonment and confiscation of property imposed on Fisher and More would have been sufficient punishment for not taking the Oath of Succession. The King, however, was intent on disposing of all who opposed him. Whilst he only makes one appearance in the play, his influence is pervasive. It is impossible that Cromwell could have proceeded against More without at least the tacit approval of Henry.

Margaret

More had four children, although only his first-born, Margaret, appears in the play. She possesses fine, intelligent qualities and is very well educated: something for which she must thank her father, who refused to distinguish between his sons and daughters when deciding on the quality of their education.

She is More's closest relation and understands his dilemmas better than any other member of the family. Her marriage to the hot-spirited Thomas Roper emphasizes her independent spirit. In the prison scene she had obviously been elected to the task of persuading More to change his mind. She tries, but is no match for him.

More

The play opens at a time of crisis for More. He had had an auspicious and highly successful career as a lawyer, writer and member of the King's Council. In 1521 he was knighted for his services to the King and was a trusted and well-loved servant.

His home in Chelsea was thronged by learned scholars, lawyers and statesmen. Even the King himself was reported to have visited him on frequent occasions.

He was a devoted father and his family has been immortalized by Holbein who painted a family group in 1526 which now hangs in the National Portrait Gallery.

In 1527 the events concerning Henry's desire to declare his marriage to Catherine invalid blew up. More felt unable to support the King but after the fall of Wolsey in 1529 he was made Chancellor.

The social and political events which lead ultimately to his execution are well defined in the play. His courage, wit and spiritual fortitude during his long trials are legendary.

He went to the scaffold in 1535 convinced that he was going to meet his God and that he had not compromised his soul in any way.

Note how More treats people. He is always gentle, always understanding, but always true to his principles. He 'reads' the characters of those around him with devastating accuracy but, seemingly, fails to recognize how low man can sink. Do you think he should have realized the strength of Henry's determination to pursue him, the lengths to which Cromwell would go and the depths to which Rich would sink, in pursuit of their individual destinies?

His relationships with Alice and Margaret are on different planes of intellectual understanding but underpinning that understanding is a deep love and respect for their individuality. There is never any indication that Alice's somewhat stolid manner causes him the slightest concern; he loves her for what she is.

Note also the incidents which demonstrate More's honesty, wit and sense of humour.

Norfolk

Norfolk is an English aristocrat with traditional views. He is a loyalist and is conservative in outlook and demeanour. He dislikes 'cleverness' but is stubborn and proud under attack. He does not understand More and is blatantly impatient with the minutiae of the legal charges brought against him. His condemnation of More is to do more with his betrayal of the fellowship of his contemporaries than opposition to his views. Norfolk simply cannot understand why More does not act in the same way as everybody else has done in order to save himself.

Rich

Rich is an early acquaintance of More's who later becomes the perjuror who brings about his execution. Rich is characterized by envy and ambition. He possesses a shallow morality which enables him to overlook the sinfulness of his acceptance of bribes under the weight of his own self-satisfaction in his public 'advancement'.

From the start it would seem that More pities him rather than being angered by his actions. Even at the end when he has perjured himself to achieve a high position, More suggests, almost pityingly, that Rich has not received much of a reward.

Roper

Roper is depicted as a young and passionate lawyer with a capacity for flirting with most of the conflicting issues in Renaissance England. Roper's temporary conversion to Lutherism enables Bolt to display More's anti-heretic sentiments. More refuses to allow Margaret to marry Roper for as long as he does not embrace Catholicism. As Margaret's husband, Roper appears rather more stable. His outspoken criticism of what he sees as More's 'sophistry' may have contributed to More taking a firm stand with the King. Roper, it seems, occasionally pricks More's conscience.

Wolsey

Wolsey was Chancellor of England under Henry. He is seen briefly in the play at a time when his fortunes are in sharp decline. Bolt depicts the ageing Chancellor as tortured by his desire to serve both King and God. More's resolute determination to remain loyal to God is a thorn in Wolsey's own conscience.

What happens in each scene

Act 1, scene 1: The action opens in More's house where he is shown to be surrounded by witty and vibrant family and friends. Richard Rich refuses to accept More's advice to become a teacher and reveals to the audience a dangerous ambition. The Duke of Norfolk arrives, full of humour, and is revealed as a bluff, energetic man, though with no high regard for intellectuals. Rich's academic knowledge is contrasted against Norfolk's rugged anti-intellectualism. More's daughter is seen as a fine, educated girl and his wife as homely and caring.

The pleasant scene is broken by mention of the unpopular Cromwell and a summons by Wolsey for More to attend an urgent meeting.

Scene 2: Wolsey attempts to persuade More to support him in getting the Pope to annul Henry's marriage to Catherine. More refuses and Wolsey announces his enmity. More says that he would prefer to be Chancellor rather than allow Cromwell to take over. Cromwell arrives to see Wolsey as More is leaving.

Scene 3: Cromwell is interested in what passed between Wolsey and More, but fails to get any information of value from More.

Chapuys, the Spanish diplomat, announces the interest of the Spanish Court in the matter of the annulment of the marriage and attempts to win More's support. More is too clever a statesman to agree to support Chapuys, and keeps his own counsel.

Scene 4: More returns home by boat to find his daughter's suitor, Roper, waiting up for him to ask for her hand in marriage. More refuses until Roper gives up his current, heretical beliefs. More's wife is aroused by Roper's departure and asks More how his interview with Wolsey has gone. More is cautious in his answers in order to protect his family from involvement in potentially dangerous State matters.

Scene 5: The Common Man announces the death of Wolsey and tells the audience of More's succession to the Chancellorship.

We next meet Cromwell at Hampton Court. Rich denies his friendship with More to Cromwell. Chapuys and Cromwell indulge in intelligence and counter-intelligence banter. Both are anxious to spy on More and both interview and bribe the Steward to inform on him. The Steward gives nothing away but is aware of the danger that his master is in.

Scene 6: At More's house there is panic in the household. More cannot be found and Alice, Margaret and Norfolk have been informed of an imminent visit by the King himself. More returns from prayer dishevelled and improperly dressed – in some people's opinion – to receive the King, who arrives in full pomp and splendour. Margaret barely escapes annoying the King with her display of education but redeems herself. Despite the fact that the King had promised not to press More about the matter of Catherine he reopens the discussion and warns More not to oppose his will in this matter. His mood has changed radically and he leaves suddenly at eight o'clock without dining with the family. More reassures his family, who fear the worst, by saying that the King had probably left to meet Anne Boleyn rather than in anger at him.

Roper has had a change of belief. Rich appears and attempts to warn More that Cromwell is spying on him. The family want Rich arrested but More resists and makes a spirited, legal argument about the dangers of breaking the law to suit personal needs. The family go in to dinner.

Scene 7: The Common Man becomes a publican and hosts a clandestine meeting between Cromwell and Rich. Cromwell promises Rich promotion in return for information against More. Rich reveals some facts about a silver goblet which More had been given as a bribe. Cromwell is determined to trap More and shows his ruthlessness and cruelty in deliberately burning Rich's hand in the final scene of the Act.

Act 2, scene 1: The Common Man announces the passage of time and reports on the establishment of the Church of England (Henry VIII's Act of Supremacy).

Roper has become a devout Catholic again and opposes More for remaining Chancellor and thus associating himself, through office, with the State's decision to break with Rome. More is awaiting news from the Convocation of Clergy. If they approve of the Act More will resign the Chancellorship. Chapuys arrives and attempts to persuade More to be his ally. At this point Norfolk breaks in with news from the Convocation and Chapuys hurriedly departs. The Convocation has capitulated and More resigns. The King has already sent a message via Norfolk accepting the resignation. More patriotically informs Norfolk of Chapuys' news that Catholics in the North are on the point of insurrection. The family prepare, with some dissatisfaction, to discharge their staff and accept a humbler station in life. More is convinced that his silence will protect him from any other attack by the State. The Steward resigns.

Scene 2: Cromwell is not content with More's silence and has been requested by the King to get a declaration of loyalty out of More. His attempt to use Rich's evidence that More has accepted bribes falls flat when Norfolk recalls that More gave away the offending silver goblet the moment he knew it was a bribe. Norfolk is required by the King to join the effort to persuade More to actually support the King's new marriage. Having failed to catch More out on one legal detail, Cromwell is determined to find another. The Common Man becomes Rich's steward.

Scene 3: More and his family are struggling with poverty when Chapuys arrives with a letter from the Spanish King, Charles. More refuses to open it and shows Margaret the unbroken seal. Chapuys leaves. More's caution extends into a refusal to accept money from the Church for his books – this refusal further angers his long-suffering wife.

Cromwell calls More to him to answer certain charges.

Scene 4: Rich has been appointed recorder to the enquiry. Cromwell fails to shake More on his association with the so-called 'Holy Maid of Kent'; More has been scrupulous in keeping witnessed letters in which he had warned her not to oppose the State. Cromwell's second charge concerns the authorship of 'A Defence of Seven Sacraments'. More is emphatic that it was the King's own work and that the King would not perjure himself. More is allowed to leave, for the moment.

Scene 5: Norfolk meets More and attempts to persuade him to support the King. His appeal is one of comradeship and friendship. More deliberately insults Norfolk in an attempt to alienate him and thus avoid implicating him in his own danger. The ruse works and Norfolk angrily retires.

Margaret and Roper arrive with news that Parliament has passed a new Act which requires all subjects to take an Oath supporting the succession of Anne Boleyn as Queen of England.

Scene 6: More and Bishop Fisher have refused to take the oath and are imprisoned in the Tower. The Common Man has become a jailer and reports on the subsequent fate of the Royal Commission. More is subjected to yet another night visit by the Commissioner. More knows that, although his silence has cost him his freedom and has led to confiscation of his entire property, he cannot be convicted of treason unless it is proved that his reasons for not signing the Oath of Succession were treasonable.

The Jailer (or Common Man) is promised fifty guineas if he reports on any treasonable outburst More may make. Cromwell orders that More's books be taken away from him, but rejects the idea of subjecting him to torture. Instead, he allows More to see his family, having made them swear to try to persuade him to take the Oath.

Scene 7:   The family's visit is short and More is grieved to see the poverty that his stand has brought them to. Margaret is on oath to try to persuade More to change his mind. She fails. Although his daughter shows some understanding of his situation, Alice does not, but nevertheless indicates that she loves him dearly and trusts him. More, frightened for his family's safety, urges them to flee the country.

Scene 8:   More is finally brought to trial on charges of high treason. He is told that Bishop Fisher has been executed. In a spirited defence of his position, More rejects Cromwell's arguments and shows that the law regards his 'silence' as indicating consent. Cromwell has obviously prepared for the possibility of losing that legal argument, and produces an illegal one that will work: Rich perjures himself to prove the case against More, and More is condemned to death. More's speech after being found guilty reveals his continued opposition to the King's marriage to Anne Boleyn.

Scene 9:   The Common Man becomes the Headsman and, after a brief farewell to Norfolk and Margaret, More is executed. He refuses the company of Archbishop Cranmer to the scaffold.

Coursework and preparing for the examination

If you wish to gain a certificate in English literature then there is no substitute for studying the text/s on which you are to be examined. If you cannot be bothered to do that, then neither this guide nor any other will be of use to you.

Here we give advice on studying the text, writing a good essay, producing coursework, and sitting the examination. However, if you meet problems you should ask your teacher for help.

Studying the text

No, not just read – study. You must read your text at least twice. Do not dismiss it if you find a first reading difficult or uninteresting. Approach the text with an open mind and you will often find a second reading more enjoyable. When you become a more experienced reader enjoyment usually follows from a close study of the text, when you begin to appreciate both what the author is saying and the skill with which it is said.

Having read the text, you must now study it. We restrict our remarks here to novels and plays, though much of what is said can also be applied to poetry.

1 You will know in full detail all the major incidents in your text, **why**, **where** and **when** they happen, **who** is involved, **what** leads up to them and what follows.

2 You must show that you have an **understanding of the story**, the **characters**, and the **main ideas** which the author is exploring.

3 In a play you must know what happens in each act, and more specifically the organization of the scene structure – how one follows from and builds upon another. Dialogue in both plays and novels is crucial. You must have a detailed knowledge of the major dialogues and soliloquies and the part they play in the development of plot, and the development and drawing of character.

4 When you write about a novel you will not normally be expected to quote or to refer to specific lines but references to incidents and characters must be given, and they must be accurate and specific.

5 In writing about a play you will be expected both to paraphrase dialogue and quote specific lines, always provided, of course, that they are actually contributing something to your essay!

To gain full marks in coursework and/or in an examination you will also be expected to show your own reaction to, and appreciation of, the text studied. The teacher or examiner always welcomes those essays which demonstrate the student's own thoughtful response to the text. Indeed, questions often specify such a requirement, so do participate in those classroom discussions, the debates, class dramatizations of all or selected parts of your text, and the many other activities which enable a class to share and grow in their understanding and feeling for literature.

Making notes
A half-hearted reading of your text, or watching the 'film of the book' will not give you the necessary knowledge to meet the above demands.

As you study the text jot down sequences of events; quotations of note; which events precede and follow the part you are studying; the characters involved; what the part being studied contributes to the plot and your understanding of character and ideas.

Write single words, phrases and short sentences which can be quickly reviewed and which will help you to gain a clear picture of the incident being studied. Make your notes neat and orderly, with headings to indicate chapter, scene, page, incident, character, etc, so that you can quickly find the relevant notes or part of the text when revising.

Writing the essay

Good essays are like good books, in miniature; they are thought about, planned, logically structured, paragraphed, have a clearly defined pattern and development of thought, and are presented clearly – and with neat writing! All of this will be to no avail if the tools you use, i.e. words, and the skill with which you put them together to form your sentences and paragraphs are severely limited.

How good is your general and literary vocabulary? Do you understand and can you make appropriate use of such terms as 'soliloquy', 'character', 'plot', 'mood', 'dramatically effective', 'comedy', 'allusion', 'humour', 'imagery', 'irony', 'paradox', 'anti-climax', 'tragedy'? These are all words which examiners have commented on as being misunderstood by students.

Do you understand 'metaphor', 'simile', 'alliteration'? Can you say what their effect is on you, the reader, and how they enable the author to express himself more effectively than by the use of a different literary device? If you cannot, you are employing your time ineffectively by using them.

You are writing an English literature essay and your writing should be literate and appropriate. Slang, colloquialisms and careless use of words are not tolerated in such essays.

Essays for coursework

The exact number of essays you will have to produce and their length will vary; it depends upon the requirements of the examination board whose course you are following, and whether you will be judged solely on coursework or on a mixture of coursework and examination.

As a guide, however your course is structured, you will be required to provide a folder containing at least ten essays, and from that folder approximately five will be selected for moderation purposes. Of those essays, one will normally have been done in class-time under conditions similar to those of an examination. The essays must cover the complete range of course requirements and be the unaided work of the student. One board specifies that these pieces of continuous writing should be a minimum of 400 words long, and another, a minimum of 500 words long. Ensure that you know what is required for your course, and do not aim for the minimum amount – write a full essay then prune it down if necessary.

Do take care over the presentation of your final folder of coursework. There are many devices on the market which will enable you to bind your work neatly, and in such a way that you can easily insert new pieces. Include a 'Contents' page and a front and back cover to keep your work clean. Ring binders are unsuitable items to hand in for **final** assessment purposes as they are much too bulky.

What sort of coursework essays will you be set? All boards lay down criteria similar to the following for the range of student response to literature that the coursework must cover.

Work must demonstrate that the student:

1 shows an understanding not only of surface meaning but also of a deeper awareness of themes and attitudes;

2 recognizes and appreciates ways in which authors use language;

3 recognizes and appreciates ways in which writers achieve their effects, particularly in how the work is structured and in its characterization;

4 can write imaginatively in exploring and developing ideas so as to communicate a sensitive and informed personal response to what is read.

Much of what is said in the section **'Writing essays in an examination'** (below) is relevant here, but for coursework essays you have the advantage of plenty of time to prepare your work–so take advantage of it.

There is no substitute for arguing, discussing and talking about a question on a particular text or theme. Your teacher should give you plenty of opportunity for this in the classroom. Listening to what others say about a subject often opens up for you new ways to look at and respond to it. The same can be said for reading about a topic. Be careful not to copy down slavishly what others say and write. Jot down notes then go away and think about what you have heard, read and written. Make more notes of your own and then start to clarify your own thoughts, feelings and emotions on the subject about which you are writing. Most students make the mistake of doing their coursework essays in a rush–you have time so use it.

Take a great deal of care in planning your work. From all your notes, write a rough draft and then start the task of really perfecting it.

1 Look at your arrangement of paragraphs, is there a logical development of thought or argument? Do the paragraphs need rearranging in order? Does the first or last sentence of any paragraph need redrafting in order to provide a sensible link with the preceding or next paragraph?

2 Look at the pattern of sentences within each paragraph. Are your thoughts and ideas clearly developed and expressed? Have you used any quotations, paraphrases, or references to incidents to support your opinions and ideas? Are those references relevant and apt, or just 'padding'?

3 Look at the words you have used. Try to avoid repeating words in close proximity one to another. Are the words you have used to comment on the text being studied the most appropriate and effective, or just the first ones you thought of?

4 Check your spelling and punctuation.

5 Now write a final draft, the quality of which should reflect the above considerations.

Writing essays in an examination
Read the question. Identify the key words and phrases. Write them down, and as they are dealt with in your essay plan, tick them off.

Plan your essay. Spend about five minutes jotting down ideas; organize your thoughts and ideas into a logical and developing order–a structure is essential to the production of a good essay. Remember, brief, essential notes only!

Write your essay
How long should it be? There is no magic length. What you must do is answer the question set, fully and sensitively in the time allowed. You will probably have about forty minutes to answer an essay question, and within that time you should produce an essay between roughly 350 and 500 words in length. Very short answers will not do justice to the question, very long answers will probably contain much irrelevant information and waste time that should be spent on the next answer.

How much quotation? Use only that which is apt and contributes to the clarity and quality of your answer. No examiner will be impressed by 'padding'.

What will the examiners be looking for in an essay?
1 An answer to the question set, and not a prepared answer to another, albeit slightly similar question done in class.

2 A well-planned, logically structured and paragraphed essay with a beginning, middle and end.

3 Accurate references to plot, character, theme, as required by the question.

4 Appropriate, brief, and if needed, frequent quotation and references to support and demonstrate the comments that you are making in your essay.

5 Evidence that reading the text has prompted in you a personal response to it, as well as some judgment and appreciation of its literary merit.

How do you prepare to do this?
1 During your course you should write between three to five essays on each text.

2 Make good use of class discussion etc, as mentioned in a previous paragraph on page 73.

3 Try to see a live performance of a play. It may help to see a film of a play or book, though be aware that directors sometimes leave out episodes, change their order, or worse, add episodes that are not in the original – so be very careful. In the end, there is no substitute for **reading and studying** the text!

Try the following exercises without referring to any notes or text.

1 Pick a character from your text.

2 Make a list of his/her qualities – both positive and negative ones, or aspects that you cannot quite define. Jot down single words to describe each quality. If you do not know the word you want, use a thesaurus, but use it in conjunction with a dictionary and make sure you are fully aware of the meaning of each word you use.

3 Write a short sentence which identifies one or more places in the text where you think each quality is demonstrated.

4 Jot down any brief quotation, paraphrase of conversation or outline of an incident which shows that quality.

5 Organize the list. Identify groupings which contrast the positive and negative aspects of character.

6 Write a description of that character which makes full use of the material you have just prepared.

7 What do you think of the character you have just described? How has he/she reacted to and coped with the pressures of the other characters, incidents, and the setting of the story? Has he/she changed in any way? In no more than 100 words, including 'evidence' taken from the text, write a balanced assessment of the character, and draw some conclusions.

You should be able to do the above without notes, and without the text, unless you are to take an examination which allows the use of plain texts. In plain text examinations you are allowed to take in a copy of your text. It must be without notes, either your own or the publisher's. The intention is to enable you to consult a text in the examination so as to confirm memory of detail, thus enabling a candidate to quote and refer more accurately in order to illustrate his/her views that more effectively. Examiners will expect a high standard of accurate reference, quotation and comment in a plain text examination.

Sitting the examination

You will have typically between two and five essays to write and you will have roughly 40 minutes, on average, to write each essay.

On each book you have studied, you should have a choice of doing at least one out of two or three essay titles set.

1 **Before sitting the exam**, make sure you are completely clear in your mind that you know exactly how many questions you must answer, which sections of the paper you must tackle, and how many questions you may, or must, attempt on any one book or in any one section of the paper. If you are not sure, ask your teacher.

2 **Always read the instructions** given at the top of your examination paper. They are

there to help you. Take your time, and try to relax – panicking will not help.

3 **Be very clear about timing, and organizing your time.**

(a) Know how long the examination is.
(b) Know how many questions you must do.
(c) Divide (b) into (a) to work out how long you may spend on each question. (Bear in mind that some questions may attract more marks, and should therefore take proportionately more time.)
(d) Keep an eye on the time, and do not spend more than you have allowed for any one question.
(e) If you have spare time at the end you can come back to a question and do more work on it.
(f) Do not be afraid to jot down notes as an aid to memory, but do cross them out carefully after use – a single line will do!

4 **Do not rush the decision** as to which question you are going to answer on a particular text.

(a) Study each question carefully.
(b) Be absolutely sure what each one is asking for.
(c) Make your decision as to which you will answer.

5 **Having decided which question** you will attempt:

(a) jot down the key points of the actual question – use single words or short phrases;
(b) think about how you are going to arrange your answer. Five minutes here, with some notes jotted down will pay dividends later;
(c) write your essay, and keep an eye on the time!

6 **Adopt the same approach** for all questions. Do write answers for the maximum number of questions you are told to attempt. One left out will lose its proportion of the total marks. Remember also, you will never be awarded extra marks, over and above those already allocated, if you write an extra long essay on a particular question.

7 **Do not waste time** on the following:

(a) an extra question – you will get no marks for it;
(b) worrying about how much anyone else is writing, they can't help you!
(c) relaxing at the end with time to spare – you do not have any. Work up to the very moment the invigilator tells you to stop writing. Check and recheck your work, including spelling and punctuation. Every single mark you gain helps, and that last mark might tip the balance between success and failure – the line has to be drawn somewhere.

8 **Help the examiner.**

(a) Do not use red or green pen or pencil on your paper. Examiners usually annotate your script in red and green, and if you use the same colours it will cause unnecessary confusion.
(b) Leave some space between each answer or section of an answer. This could also help you if you remember something you wish to add to your answer when you are checking it.
(c) Number your answers as instructed. If it is question 3 you are doing, do not label it 'C'.
(d) Write neatly. It will help you to communicate effectively with the examiner who is trying to read your script.

Glossary of literary terms

Mere knowledge of the words in this list or other specialist words used when studying literature is not sufficient. You must know when to use a particular term, and be able to describe what it contributes to that part of the work which is being discussed.

For example, merely to label something as being a metaphor does not help an examiner or teacher to assess your response to the work being studied. You must go on to analyse what the literary device contributes to the work. Why did the author use a metaphor at all? Why not some other literary device? What extra sense of feeling or meaning does the metaphor convey to the reader? How effective is it in supporting the author's intention? What was the author's intention, as far as you can judge, in using that metaphor?

Whenever you use a particular literary term you must do so with a purpose and that purpose usually involves an explanation and expansion upon its use. Occasionally you will simply use a literary term 'in passing', as, for example, when you refer to the 'narrator' of a story as opposed to the 'author' – they are not always the same! So please be sure that you understand both the meaning and purpose of each literary term you employ.

This list includes only those words which we feel will assist in helping you to understand the major concepts in play and novel construction. It makes no attempt to be comprehensive. These are the concepts which examiners frequently comment upon as being inadequately grasped by many students. Your teacher will no doubt expand upon this list and introduce you to other literary devices and words within the context of the particular work/s you are studying – the most useful place to experience and explore them and their uses.

Plot This is the plan or story of a play or novel. Just as a body has a skeleton to hold it together, so the plot forms the 'bare bones' of the work of literature in play or novel form. It is however, much more than this. It is arranged in time, so one of the things which encourages us to continue reading is to see what happens next. It deals with causality, that is how one event or incident causes another. It has a sequence, so that in general, we move from the beginning through to the end.

Structure The arrangement and interrelationship of parts in a play or novel are obviously bound up with the plot. An examination of how the author has structured his work will lead us to consider the function of, say, the 43 letters which are such an important part of *Pride and Prejudice*. We would consider the arrangement of the time-sequence in *Wuthering Heights* with its 'flashbacks' and their association with the different narrators of the story. In a play we would look at the scene divisions and how different events are placed in a relationship so as to produce a particular effect; where soliloquies occur so as to inform the audience of a character's innermost emotions and feelings. Do be aware that great works of fiction are not just simply thrown together by their authors. We study a work in detail, admiring its parts and the intricacies of its structure. The reason for a work's greatness has to do with the genius of its author and the care of its construction. Ultimately, though, we do well to remember that it is the work as a whole that we have to judge, not just the parts which make up that whole.

Narrator   A narrator tells or relates a story. In *Wuthering Heights* various characters take on the task of narrating the events of the story: Cathy, Heathcliff, etc, as well as being, at other times, central characters taking their part in the story. Sometimes the author will be there, as it were, in person, relating and explaining events. The method adopted in telling the story relates very closely to style and structure.

Style   The manner in which something is expressed or performed, considered as separate from its intrinsic content or meaning. It might well be that a lyrical, almost poetical style will be used, for example concentrating on the beauties and contrasts of the natural world as a foil to the narration of the story and creating emotions in the reader which serve to heighten reactions to the events being played out on the page. It might be that the author uses a terse, almost staccato approach to the conveyance of his story. There is no simple route to grasping the variations of style which are to be found between different authors or indeed within one novel. The surest way to appreciate this difference is to read widely and thoughtfully and to analyse and appreciate the various strategies which an author uses to command our attention.

Character   A person represented in a play or story. However, the word also refers to the combination of traits and qualities distinguishing the individual nature of a person or thing. Thus, a characteristic is one such distinguishing quality: in *Pride and Prejudice*, the pride and prejudices of various characters are central to the novel, and these characteristics which are associated with Mr Darcy, Elizabeth, and Lady Catherine in that novel, enable us to begin assessing how a character is reacting to the surrounding events and people. Equally, the lack of a particular trait or characteristic can also tell us much about a character.

Character development   In *Pride and Prejudice*, the extent to which Darcy's pride, or Elizabeth's prejudice is altered, the recognition by those characters of such change, and the events of the novel which bring about the changes are central to any exploration of how a character develops, for better or worse.

Irony   This is normally taken to be the humorous or mildly sarcastic use of words to imply the opposite of what they say. It also refers to situations and events and thus you will come across references such as prophetic, tragic, and dramatic irony.

Dramatic irony   This occurs when the implications of a situation or speech are understood by the audience but not by all or some of the characters in the play or novel. We also class as ironic words spoken innocently but which a later event proves either to have been mistaken or to have prophesied that event. When we read in the play *Macbeth*:

> *Macbeth*
> Tonight we hold a solemn supper, sir,
> And I'll request your presence.

> *Banquo*
> Let your highness
> Command upon me, to the which my duties
> Are with a most indissoluble tie
> Forever knit.

we, as the audience, will shortly have revealed to us the irony of Macbeth's words. He does not expect Banquo to attend the supper as he plans to have Banquo murdered before the supper occurs. However, what Macbeth does not know is the prophetic irony of Banquo's response. His 'duties. . . a most indissoluble tie' will be fulfilled by his appearance at the supper as a ghost – something Macbeth certainly did not forsee or welcome, and which Banquo most certainly did not have in mind!

Tragedy   This is usually applied to a play in which the main character, usually a person of importance and outstanding personal qualities, falls to disaster through the combination of personal failing and circumstances with which he cannot deal. Such tragic happenings may also be central to a novel. In *The Mayor of Casterbridge*, flaws in Henchard's character are partly responsible for his downfall and eventual death.

In Shakespeare's plays, *Macbeth* and *Othello*, the tragic heroes from which the two plays take their names, are both highly respected and honoured men who have proven their outstanding personal qualities. Macbeth, driven on by his ambition and that of his very determined wife, kills his king. It leads to civil war in his country, to his own eventual downfall and death, and to his wife's suicide. Othello, driven to an insane jealousy by the cunning of his lieutenant, Iago, murders his own innocent wife and commits suicide.

Satire Where topical issues, folly or evil are held up to scorn by means of ridicule and irony – the satire may be subtle or openly abusive.

In *Animal Farm*, George Orwell used the rebellion of the animals against their oppressive owner to satirize the excesses of the Russian revolution at the beginning of the 20th century. It would be a mistake, however, to see the satire as applicable only to that event. There is a much wider application of that satire to political and social happenings both before and since the Russian revolution and in all parts of the world.

Images An image is a mental representation or picture. One that constantly recurs in *Macbeth* is clothing, sometimes through double meanings of words: 'he seems rapt withal', 'Why do you dress me in borrowed robes?', 'look how our partner's rapt', 'Like our strange garments, cleave not to their mould', 'Whiles I stood rapt in the wonder of it', 'which would be worn now in their newest gloss', 'Was the hope drunk Wherein you dressed yourself?', 'Lest our old robes sit easier than our new.', 'like a giant's robe upon a dwarfish thief'. All these images serve to highlight and comment upon aspects of Macbeth's behaviour and character. In Act 5, Macbeth the loyal soldier who was so honoured by his king at the start of the play, struggles to regain some small shred of his self-respect. Three times he calls to Seyton for his armour, and finally moves toward his destiny with the words 'Blow wind, come wrack, At least we'll die with harness on our back' – his own armour, not the borrowed robes of a king he murdered.

Do remember that knowing a list of images is not sufficient. You must be able to interpret them and comment upon the contribution they make to the story being told.

Theme A unifying idea, image or motif, repeated or developed throughout a work.

In *Pride and Prejudice*, a major theme is marriage. During the course of the novel we are shown various views of and attitudes towards marriage. We actually witness the relationships of four different couples through their courtship, engagement and eventual marriage. Through those events and the examples presented to us in the novel of other already married couples, the author engages in a thorough exploration of the theme.

This list is necessarily short. There are whole books devoted to the explanation of literary terms. Some concepts, like style, need to be experienced and discussed in a group setting with plenty of examples in front of you. Others, such as dramatic irony, need keen observation from the student and a close knowledge of the text to appreciate their significance and existence. All such specialist terms are well worth knowing. But they should be used only if they enable you to more effectively express your knowledge and appreciation of the work being studied.

Titles in the series

Pride and Prejudice

Animal Farm

To Kill A Mockingbird

Lord of the Flies

Romeo and Juliet

A Man for All Seasons

The Mayor of Casterbridge

Of Mice and Men

Macbeth

Great Expectations

Far From the Madding Crowd

Jane Eyre